O'REILLY®
Strata
Making Data Work

Learn how to turn data into decisions.

From startups to the Fortune 500, smart companies are betting on data-driven insight, seizing the opportunities that are emerging from the convergence of four powerful trends:

- New methods of collecting, managing, and analyzing data

- Cloud computing that offers inexpensive storage and flexible, on-demand computing power for massive data sets

- Visualization techniques that turn complex data into images that tell a compelling story

- Tools that make the power of data available to anyone

Get control over big data and turn it into insight with O'Reilly's Strata offerings. Find the inspiration and information to create new products or revive existing ones, understand customer behavior, and get the data edge.

T0256858

O'REILLY®

Visit oreilly.com/data to learn more.

Machine Learning for Email

Drew Conway and John Myles White

O'REILLY®

Beijing · Cambridge · Farnham · Köln · Sebastopol · Tokyo

Machine Learning for Email
by Drew Conway and John Myles White

Published by O'Reilly Media, Inc., 1005 Gravenstein Highway North, Sebastopol, CA 95472.

O'Reilly books may be purchased for educational, business, or sales promotional use. Online editions are also available for most titles (*http://my.safaribooksonline.com*). For more information, contact our corporate/institutional sales department: (800) 998-9938 or *corporate@oreilly.com*.

Editor: Julie Steele	**Cover Designer:** Karen Montgomery
Production Editor: Kristen Borg	**Interior Designer:** David Futato
Proofreader: O'Reilly Production Services	**Illustrator:** Robert Romano

Revision History for the First Edition:

    2011-10-24   First release

See *http://oreilly.com/catalog/errata.csp?isbn=9781449314309* for release details.

ISBN: 978-1-449-31430-9

[LSI]

1319208133

Table of Contents

Preface

Machine Learning for Hackers: Email

To explain the perspective from which this book was written, it will be helpful to define the terms *machine learning* and *hackers*.

What is machine learning? At the highest level of abstraction, we can think of machine learning as a set of tools and methods that attempt to infer patterns and extract insight from a record of the observable world. For example, if we're trying to teach a computer to recognize the zip codes written on the fronts of envelopes, our data may consist of photographs of the envelopes along with a record of the zip code that each envelope was addressed to. That is, within some context we can take a record of the actions of our subjects, learn from this record, and then create a model of these activities that will inform our understanding of this context going forward. In practice, this requires data, and in contemporary applications this often means a lot of data (several terabytes). Most machine learning techniques take the availability of such a data set as given—which, in light of the quantities of data that are produced in the course of running modern companies, means new opportunities.

What is a hacker? Far from the stylized depictions of nefarious teenagers or Gibsonian cyber-punks portrayed in pop culture, we believe a hacker is someone who likes to solve problems and experiment with new technologies. If you've ever sat down with the latest O'Reilly book on a new computer language and knuckled out code until you were well past "Hello, World," then you're a hacker. Or, if you've dismantled a new gadget until you understood the entire machinery's architecture, then we probably mean you, too. These pursuits are often undertaken for no other reason than to have gone through the process and gained some knowledge about the *how* and *the why* of an unknown technology.

Along with an innate curiosity for how things work and a desire to build, a computer hacker (as opposed to a car hacker, life hacker, food hacker, etc.) has experience with software design and development. This is someone who has written programs before, likely in many different languages. To a hacker, UNIX is not a four-letter word, and command-line navigation and bash operations may come as naturally as working with windowing operating systems. Using regular expressions and tools such as sed, awk and grep are a hacker's first line of defense when dealing with text. In the chapters of this book, we will assume a relatively high level of this sort of knowledge.

How This Book is Organized

Machine learning exists at the intersection of traditional mathematics and statistics with software engineering and computer science. As such, there are many ways to learn the discipline. Considering its theoretical foundations in mathematics and statistics, newcomers would do well to attain some degree of mastery of the formal specifications of basic machine learning techniques. There are many excellent books that focus on the fundamentals, the seminal work being Hastie, Tibshirani, and Friedman's *The Elements of Statistical Learning* [HTF09].* But another important part of the hacker mantra is to learn by doing. Many hackers may be more comfortable thinking of problems in terms of the *process* by which a solution is attained, rather than the *theoretical foundation* from which the solution is derived.

From this perspective, an alternative approach to teaching machine learning would be to use "cookbook" style examples. To understand how a recommendation system works, for example, we might provide sample training data and a version of the model, and show how the latter uses the former. There are many useful texts of this kind as well—Toby Segaran's *Programming Collective Intelligence* is an recent example [Seg07]. Such a discussion would certainly address the *how* of a hacker's method of learning, but perhaps less of the *why*. Along with understanding the mechanics of a method, we may also want to learn why it is used in a certain context or to address a specific problem.

To provide a more complete reference on machine learning for hackers, therefore, we need to compromise between providing a deep review of the theoretical foundations of the discipline and a broad exploration of its applications. To accomplish this, we have decided to teach machine learning through selected case studies.

For that reason, each chapter of this book is a self-contained case study focusing on a specific problem in machine learning. The case studies in this book will focus on a single corpus of text data from email. This corpus will be used to explore techniques for classification and ranking of these messages.

---

* *The Elements of Statistical Learning* can now be downloaded free of charge at *http://www-stat.stanford.edu/~tibs/ElemStatLearn/*.

The primary tool we will use to explore these case studies is the R statistical programming language (*http://www.r-project.org/*). R is particularly well suited for machine learning case studies because it is a high-level, functional, scripting language designed for data analysis. Much of the underlying algorithmic scaffolding required is already built into the language, or has been implemented as one of the thousands of R packages available on the Comprehensive R Archive Network (CRAN).[†] This will allow us to focus on the *how* and the *why* of these problems, rather than reviewing and rewriting the foundational code for each case.

Conventions Used in This Book

The following typographical conventions are used in this book:

Italic
> Indicates new terms, URLs, email addresses, filenames, and file extensions.

`Constant width`
> Used for program listings, as well as within paragraphs to refer to program elements such as variable or function names, databases, data types, environment variables, statements, and keywords.

`Constant width bold`
> Shows commands or other text that should be typed literally by the user.

`Constant width italic`
> Shows text that should be replaced with user-supplied values or by values determined by context.

 This icon signifies a tip, suggestion, or general note.

 This icon indicates a warning or caution.

Using Code Examples

This book is here to help you get your job done. In general, you may use the code in this book in your programs and documentation. You do not need to contact us for permission unless you're reproducing a significant portion of the code. For example, writing a program that uses several chunks of code from this book does not require

---

[†] For more information on CRAN, see *http://cran.r-project.org/*.

permission. Selling or distributing a CD-ROM of examples from O'Reilly books does require permission. Answering a question by citing this book and quoting example code does not require permission. Incorporating a significant amount of example code from this book into your product's documentation does require permission.

We appreciate, but do not require, attribution. An attribution usually includes the title, author, publisher, and ISBN. For example: "*Machine Learning for Email* by Drew Conway and John Myles White (O'Reilly). Copyright 2012 Drew Conway and John Myles White, 978-1-449-31430-9."

If you feel your use of code examples falls outside fair use or the permission given above, feel free to contact us at *permissions@oreilly.com*.

Safari® Books Online

Safari⠂⠄ Safari Books Online is an on-demand digital library that lets you easily
Books Online search over 7,500 technology and creative reference books and videos to find the answers you need quickly.

With a subscription, you can read any page and watch any video from our library online. Read books on your cell phone and mobile devices. Access new titles before they are available for print, and get exclusive access to manuscripts in development and post feedback for the authors. Copy and paste code samples, organize your favorites, download chapters, bookmark key sections, create notes, print out pages, and benefit from tons of other time-saving features.

O'Reilly Media has uploaded this book to the Safari Books Online service. To have full digital access to this book and others on similar topics from O'Reilly and other publishers, sign up for free at *http://my.safaribooksonline.com*.

How to Contact Us

Please address comments and questions concerning this book to the publisher:

O'Reilly Media, Inc.
1005 Gravenstein Highway North
Sebastopol, CA 95472
800-998-9938 (in the United States or Canada)
707-829-0515 (international or local)
707-829-0104 (fax)

We have a web page for this book, where we list errata, examples, and any additional information. You can access this page at:

http://oreilly.com/catalog/0636920022350

To comment or ask technical questions about this book, send email to:

bookquestions@oreilly.com

For more information about our books, courses, conferences, and news, see our website at *http://www.oreilly.com.*

Find us on Facebook: *http://facebook.com/oreilly*

Follow us on Twitter: *http://twitter.com/oreillymedia*

Watch us on YouTube: *http://www.youtube.com/oreillymedia*

## CHAPTER 1

Using R

Machine learning exists at the intersection of traditional mathematics and statistics with software engineering and computer science. In this book, we will describe several tools from traditional statistics that allow you to make sense of that world. Statistics has almost always been concerned with learning something interpretable from data, while machine learning has been concerned with turning data into something practical and usable. This contrast makes it easier to understand the term *machine learning*: Machine learning is concerned with teaching *computers* something about the world, so that they can use that knowledge to perform other tasks, while statistics is more concerned with developing tools for teaching *humans* something about the world, so that they can think more clearly about the world in order to make better decisions.

In machine learning, the *learning* occurs by extracting as much information from the data as possible (or reasonable) through algorithms that parse the basic structure of the data and distinguish the signal from the noise. After they have found the signal, or *pattern*, the algorithms simply decide that everything else that's left over is noise. For that reason, machine learning techniques are also referred to as *pattern recognition algorithms*. We can "train" our machines to learn about how data is generated in a given context, which allows us to use these algorithms to automate many useful tasks. This is where the term *training set* comes from, referring to the set of data used to build a machine learning process. The notion of observing data, learning from it, and then automating some process of recognition is at the heart of machine learning, and forms the primary arc of this book.

In this book, we will assume a relatively high degree of knowledge in basic programming techniques and algorithmic paradigms. That said, R remains a relatively niche language even among experienced programmers. In an effort to start everyone at the same starting point, this chapter will also provide some basic information on how to get started using the R language. Later in the chapter we will work through a specific example of using the R language to perform common tasks associated with machine learning.

This chapter does not provide a complete introduction to the R programming language. As you might expect, no such introduction could fit into a single book chapter. Instead, this chapter is meant to prepare the reader for the tasks associated with doing machine learning in R. Specifically, we describe the process of loading, exploring, cleaning, and analyzing data. There are many excellent resources on R that discuss language fundamentals; such as data types, arithmetic concepts, and coding best practices. Insofar as those topics are relevant to the case studies presented here, we will touch on all of these issues; however, there will be no explicit discussion of these topics. Some of these resources are listed in Table 1-1.

If you have never seen the language and its syntax before, we highly recommend going through this introduction to get some exposure. Unlike other high-level scripting languages, such as Python or Ruby, R has a unique and somewhat prickly syntax and tends to have a steeper learning curve than other languages. If you have used R before, but not in the context of machine learning, there is still value in taking the time to go through this review before moving onto the cases.

R for Machine Learning

R is a language and environment for statistical computing and graphics...R provides a wide variety of statistical (linear and nonlinear modeling, classical statistical tests, time-series analysis, classification, clustering, ...) and graphical techniques, and is highly extensible. The S language is often the vehicle of choice for research in statistical methodology, and R provides an Open Source route to participation in that activity.

—The R Project for Statistical Computing, *http://www.r-project.org/*

The best thing about R is that it was developed by statisticians. The worst thing about R is that...it was developed by statisticians.

—Bo Cowgill, Google, Inc.

R is an extremely powerful language for manipulating and analyzing data. Its meteoric rise in popularity within the data science and machine learning communities has made it the de facto lingua franca for analytics. R's success in the data analysis community stems from two factors described in the epitaphs above: R provides most of the technical power that statisticians require built into the default language, and R has been supported by a community of statisticians who are also open source devotees.

There are many technical advantages afforded by a language designed specifically for statistical computing. As the description from the R Project notes, the language provides an open-source bridge to S, which contains many highly-specialized statistical operations as base functions. For example, to perform a basic linear regression in R, one must simply pass the data to the lm function, which then returns an object containing detailed information about the regression (coefficients, standard errors, residual values, etc.). This data can then be visualized by passing the results to the `plot` function, which is designed to visualize the results of this analysis.

In other languages with large scientific computing communities, such as Python, duplicating the functionality of `lm` requires the use of several third-party libraries to represent the data (NumPy), perform the analysis (SciPy) and visualize the results (matplotlib). As we will see in the following chapters, such sophisticated analyses can be performed with a single line of code in R.

In addition, as in other scientific computing environments, the fundamental data type in R is a vector. Vectors can be aggregated and organized in various ways, but at the core, all data are represented this way. This relatively rigid perspective on data structures can be limiting, but is also logical given the application of the language. The most frequently used data structure in R is the *data frame*, which can be thought of as a matrix with attributes, an internally defined "spreadsheet" structure, or relational database-like structure in the core of the language. Fundamentally, a data frame is simply a column-wise aggregation of vectors that R affords specific functionality to, which makes it ideal for working with any manner of data.

For all of its power, R also has its disadvantages. R does not scale well with large data, and while there have been many efforts to address this problem, it remains a serious issue. For the purposes of the case studies we will review, however, this will not be an issue. The data sets we will use are relatively small, and all of the systems we will build are prototypes or proof-of-concept models. This distinction is important, because if your intention is to build enterprise level machine learning systems at the Google or Facebook scale, then R is not the right solution. In fact, companies like Google and Facebook often use R as their "data sandbox," to play with data and experiment with new machine learning methods. If one of those experiments bears fruit, then the engineers will attempt to replicate the functionality designed in R in a more appropriate language, such as C.

This ethos of experimentation has also engendered a great sense of community around the language. The social advantages of R hinge on this large and growing community of experts using and contributing to the language. As Bo Cowgill alludes to, R was borne out of statisticians' desire to have a computing environment that met their specific needs. Many R users, therefore, are experts in their various fields. This includes an extremely diverse set of disciplines, including mathematics, statistics, biology, chemistry, physics, psychology, economics, and political science, to name a few. This community of experts has built a massive collection of packages on top of the extensive base functions in R. At the time of writing, CRAN contained over 2,800 packages. In the case studies that follow, we will use many of the most popular packages, but this will only scratch the surface of what is possible with R.

Finally, while the latter portion of Cowgill's statement may seem a bit menacing, it further highlights the strength of the R community. As we will see, the R language has a particularly odd syntax that is rife with coding "gotchas" that can drive even experienced developers away. But all grammatical grievances with a language can eventually be overcome, especially for persistent hackers. What is more difficult for non-statisticians is the liberal assumption of familiarity with statistical and mathematical methods built into R functions. Using the lm function as an example, if you had never performed a linear regression, you would not know to look for coefficients, standard errors, or residual values in the results. Nor would you know how to interpret those results.

But, because the language is open source, you are always able to look at the code of a function to see exactly what it is doing. Part of what we will attempt to accomplish with this book is to explore many of these functions in the context of machine learning, but that will ultimately only address a tiny subset of what you can do in R. Fortunately, the R community is full of people willing to help you understand not only the language, but also the methods implemented in it. Table 1-1 lists some of the best places to start.

Table 1-1. Community resources for R help

Resource	Location	Description
RSeek	http://rseek.org/	When the core development team decided to create an open-source version of S and call it R, they had not considered how hard it would be to search for documents related to a single-letter language on the Web. This specialized search tool attempts to alleviate this by providing a focused portal to R documentation and information.
Official R mailing lists	http://www.r-project.org/mail.html	There are several listservs dedicated to the R language, including announcements, packages, development—and of course—help. Many of the language's core developers frequent these lists, and responses are often quick and terse.
StackOverflow	http://stackoverflow.com/questions/tagged/r	Hackers will know StackOverflow.com as one of the premier web resources for coding tips in any language, and the R tag is no exception. Thanks to the efforts of several prominent R community members, there is an active and vibrant collection of experts adding and answering R questions on StackOverflow.
#rstats Twtter hash-tag	http://search.twitter.com/search?q=%23rstats	There is also a very active community of R users on Twitter, and they have adopted the #rstats hashtag as their signifier. The thread is a great place to find links to useful resources, find experts in the language, and post questions—as long as they can fit into 140 characters!

Resource	Location	Description
R-Bloggers	*http://www.r-bloggers.com/*	There are hundreds of people blogging about how they use R in their research, work, or just for fun. R-bloggers.com aggregates these blogs and provides a single source for all things related to R in the blogosphere, and is a great place to learn by example.
Video Rchive	*http://www.vcasmo.com/user/drewconway*	As the R community grows, so too do the number of regional meetups and gatherings related to the language. The Rchive attempts to document the presentations and tutorials given at these meetings by posting videos and slides, and now contains presentations from community members all over the world.

The remainder of this chapter focuses on getting you set up with R and using it. This includes downloading and installing R, as well as installing R packages. We conclude with a miniature case study that will serve as an introduction to some of the R idioms we'll use in later chapters. This includes issues of loading, cleaning, organizing, and analyzing data.

Downloading and Installing R

Like many open source projects, R is distributed by a series of regional mirrors. If you do not have R already installed on your machine, the first step is to download it. Go to *http://cran.r-project.org/mirrors.html* and select the CRAN mirror closest to you. Once you have selected a mirror, you will need to download the appropriate distribution of R for whichever operating system you are running.

R relies on several legacy libraries compiled from C and Fortran. As such, depending on your operating system and your familiarity with installing software from source code, you may choose whether to install R from a compiled binary distribution or the source. Below, we present instruction for installing R on Windows, Mac OS X, and Linux distributions, with notes on installing from either source or binaries when available.

Finally, R is available in both 32- and 64-bit versions and, depending on your hardware and operating system combination, you should install the appropriate version.

Windows

For Windows operating systems there are two subdirectories available to install R: base and contrib. The latter is a directory of compiled Windows binary versions of the all of the contributed R packages in CRAN, while the former is the basic installation. Select the base installation, and download the latest compiled binary. Installing contributed packages is easy to do from R itself and is not language-specific; therefore, it is not necessary to to install anything from the `contrib` directory. Follow the on-screen instructions for the installation.

Once the installation has successfully completed, you will have an R application in your Start menu, which will open the RGui and R Console, as pictured in Figure 1-1.

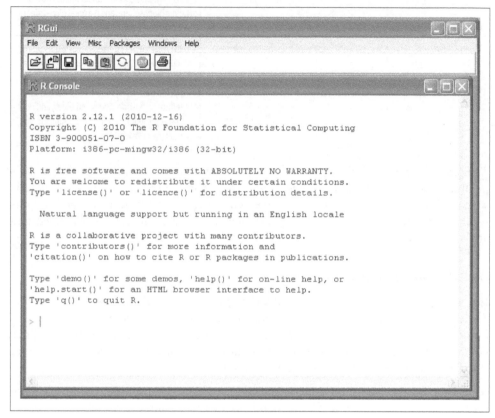

Figure 1-1. The RGui and R console on a Windows installation

For most standard Windows installations, this process should proceed without any issues. If you have a customized installation, or encounter errors during the installation, consult the *R for Windows FAQ* at your mirror of choice.

Mac OS X

Fortunately for Mac OS X users, R comes pre-installed with the operating system. You can check this by opening the `Terminal.app` and simply typing R at the command-line. You are now ready to begin! For some users, however, it will be useful to have a GUI application to interact with the R console. For this you will need to install separate software. With Mac OS X, you have the option of installing from either a compiled binary or the source. To install from a binary—recommended for users with no experience using a Linux command line—simply download the latest version at your mirror of choice at *http://cran.r-project.org/mirrors.html* and following the on-screen instructions. Once the installation is complete, you will have both R.app (32-bit) and R64.app (64-bit) available in your Applications folder. Depending on your version of Mac OS X and your machine's hardware, you may choose which version you wish to work with.

As with the Windows installation, if you are installing from binary this process should proceed without any problems. When you open your new R application you will see a console similar to the one pictured in Figure 1-2.

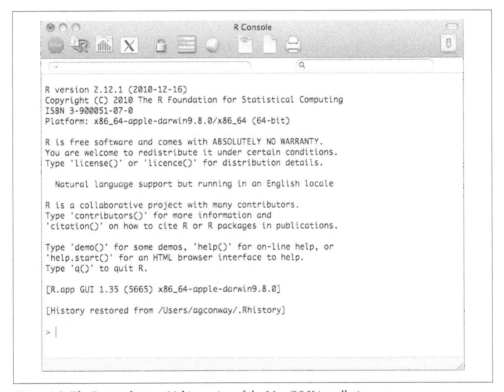

Figure 1-2. *The R console on a 64-bit version of the Mac OS X installation*

 If you have a custom installation of Mac OS X or wish to customize the installation of R for your particular configuration, we recommend that you install from the source code. To install R from source on Mac OS X requires both C and Fortran compilers, which are not included in the standard installation of the operating system. You can install these compilers using the Mac OS X Developers Tools DVD included with your original Mac OS X installation package, or you can install the necessary compilers from the *tools* directory at the mirror of your choice.

Once you have all of the necessary compilers to install from source, the process is the typical configure, make, and install procedure used to install most software at the command line. Using the `Terminal.app`, navigate to the folder with the source code and execute the following commands:

```
$ ./configure
$ make
$ make install
```

Depending on your permission settings, you may have to invoke the `sudo` command as a prefix to the configuration step and provide your system password. If you encounter any errors during the installation, using either the compiled binary distribution or the source code, consult the *R for Mac OS X FAQ* at the mirror of your choice.

Linux

As with Mac OS X, R comes preinstalled on many Linux distributions. Simply type `R` at the command line and the R console will be loaded. You can now begin programming! The CRAN mirror also includes installations specific to several Linux distributions, with instructions for installing R on Debian, RedHat, SUSE, and Ubuntu. If you use one of these installations, we recommend that you consult the instructions for your operating system, because there is considerable variance in the best practices between Linux distributions.

IDEs and Text Editors

R is a scripting language and therefore the majority of the work done in this book's case studies will be done within a IDE or text editor, rather than directly inputted into the R console. As we will show in the next section, some tasks are well suited for the console, such as package installation, but primarily you will want to be working within the IDE or text editor of your choice.

For those running the GUI in either Windows or Mac OS X, there is a basic text editor available from that application. By navigating to *File→New Document* from the menu bar, or clicking on the blank document icon in the header of the window (highlighted in Figure 1-3), you will open a blank document in the text editor. As a hacker, you likely already have an IDE or text editor of choice, and we recommend that you use whichever environment you are most comfortable in for the case studies. There are simply too many options to enumerate here, and we have no intention of inserting ourselves in the infamous `emacs` versus `vim` debate.

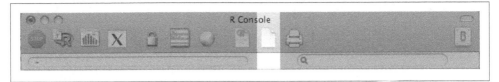

Figure 1-3. Text editor icon in R GUI

Loading and Installing R Packages

There are many well-designed, maintained, and supported R packages related to machine learning. Loading packages in R is very straightforward. There are two functions to perform this: `library` and `require`. There are some subtle differences between the two, but for the purposes of this book, the primary difference is that `require` will return a Boolean (`TRUE` or `FALSE`) value, indicating whether the package is installed on the machine after attempting to load it. As an example, below we use `library` to load `spatstat` but `require` for `lda`. By using the `print` function, we can see that we have `lda` installed because a Boolean value of `TRUE` was returned after the package was loaded:

```
library(spatstat)
print(require(lda))
[1] TRUE
```

If we did not have `lda` installed (i.e., `FALSE` was returned by `require`), then we would need to install that package before proceeding.

 If you are working with a fresh installation of R, then you will have to install a number of packages to complete all of the case studies in this book.

There are two ways to install packages in R; either with the GUI interface or with the `install.packages` function from the console. Given the intended audience for this book, we will be interacting with R exclusively from the console during the case studies, but it is worth pointing out how to use the GUI interface to install packages. From the menu bar in the application, navigate to *Packages &Data→Package Installer*, and a window will appear as displayed in Figure 1-4. From the *Package Repository* drop-down, select either *CRAN (binaries)* or *CRAN (sources)* and click the *Get List* button to load all of the packages available for installation. The most recent version of packages will be available in the *CRAN (sources)* repository, and if you have the necessary compilers installed on your machine, we recommend using the sources repository. You can now select the package you wish to install and click *Install Selected* to install the packages.

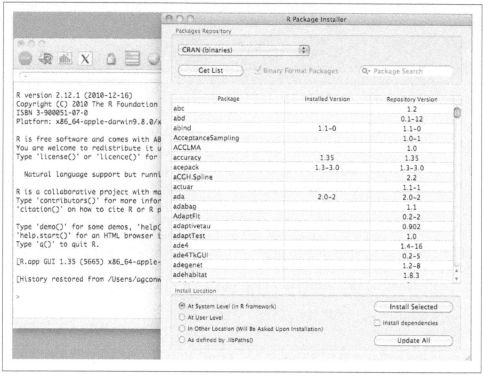

Figure 1-4. Installing R packages using the GUI interface

The `install.packages` function is the preferred way to install packages because it provides greater flexibility in how and where packages get installed. One of the primary advantages of using `install.packages` is that it allows you to install from local source code as well as from CRAN. Though uncommon, occasionally you may may want to install a package that is not yet available on CRAN—for example, if you're updating to an experimental version of a package. In these cases you will need to install from source:

```
install.packages("tm", dependencies=TRUE)
setwd("~/Downloads/")
install.packages("RCurl_1.5-0.tar.gz", repos=NULL, type="source")
```

In the first example above, we use the default settings to install the `tm` package from CRAN. The `tm` provides function used to do text mining, and we will use it in Chapter 3 to perform classification on email text. One useful parameter in the `install.packages` function is `suggests`, which by default is set to `FALSE` but if activated will instruct the function to download and install any secondary packages used by the primary installation. As a best practice, we recommend always setting this to `TRUE`, especially if you are working with a clean installation of R.

Alternatively, we can also install directly from compressed source files. In the example above, we are installing the `RCurl` package from the source code available on the author's website. Using the `setwd` function to make sure the R working directory is set to the directory where the source file has been saved, we can simply execute the above command to install directly from the source code. Note the two parameters that have been altered in this case. First, we must tell the function not to use one of the CRAN repositories by setting `repos=NULL`, and specify the type of installation using `type="source"`.

As mentioned, we will use several packages through the course of this text. Table 1-2 lists all of the packages used in the case studies and includes a brief description of their purpose, along with a link to additional information about each.

We are now ready to begin exploring machine learning with R! Before we proceed to the case studies, however, we will review some R functions and operations that we will use frequently.

Table 1-2. R packages used in this book

Name	Location	Author	Description & Use
ggplot2	http://had.co .nz/ggplot2/	Hadley Wick-ham	An implementation of the grammar of graphics in R. The premier package for creating high-quality graphics.
plyr	http://had.co .nz/plyr/	Hadley Wick-ham	A set of tools used to manipulate, aggregate and manage data in R.
tm	http://www .spatstat.org/ spatstat/	Ingo Feinerer	A collection of functions for performing text mining in R. Used to work with unstructured text data.

R Basics for Machine Learning

UFO Sightings in the United States, from 1990-2010

As we stated at the outset, we believe that the best way to learn a new technical skill is to start with a problem you wish to solve or a question you wish to answer. Being excited about the higher level vision of your work makes makes learning from case studies work. In this review of basic concepts in the R language, we will not be addressing a machine learning problem, but we will encounter several issues related to working with data and managing it in R. As we will see in the case studies, quite often we will spend the bulk of our time getting the data formatted and organized in a way that suits the analysis. Very little time, in terms of coding, is usually spent running the analysis.

For this case we will address a question with pure entertainment value. Recently, the data service Infochimps.com (*http://www.infochimps.com*) released a data set with over 60,000 documented reports of unidentified flying objects (UFO) sightings. The data spans hundreds of years and has reports from all over the world. Though it is international, the majority of sightings in the data come from the United States. With the time and spatial dimensions of the data, one question we might ask is: are there seasonal trends in UFO sightings; and what, if any, variation is there among UFO sightings across the different states in the U.S.?

This is a great data set to start exploring, because it is rich, well-structured, and fun to work with. It is also useful for this exercise because it is a large text file, which is typically the type of data we will deal with in this book. In such text files there are often messy parts, so we will use base functions in R and some external libraries to clean and organize the raw data. This section will take you step-by-step through an entire simple analysis that tries to answer the questions we posed earlier. You will find the code for this section in the code folder for this chapter as the ufo_sightings.R file. We begin by loading the data and required libraries for the analysis.

Loading libraries and the data

First, we will load the ggplot2 package, which we will use in the final steps of our visual analysis:

```
library(ggplot2)
```

While loading ggplot2, you will notice that this package also loads two other required packages: plyr and reshape. Both of these packages are used for manipulating and organizing data in R, and we will use plyr in this example to aggregate and organize the data.

The next step is to load the data into R from the text file ufo_awesome.tsv, which is located in data/ufo/ directory for this chapter. Note that the file is tab-delimited (hence the .tsv file extension), which means we will need to use the read.delim function to load the data. Because R exploits defaults very heavily, we have to be particularly conscientious of the default parameter settings for the functions we use in our scripts. To see how we can learn about parameters in R, suppose that we had never used the read.delim function before and needed to read the help files. Alternatively, assume that we do not know that read.delim exists and need to find a function to read delimited data into a data frame. R offers several useful functions for searching for help:

```
?read.delim               # Access a function's help file
??base::delim             # Search for 'delim' in all help files for functions
                          # in 'base'
help.search("delimited")  # Search for 'delimited' in all help files
RSiteSearch("parsing text")  # Search for the term 'parsing text' on the R site.
```

In the first example, we append a question mark to the beginning of the function. This will open the help file for the given function and it's an extremely useful R shortcut. We can also search for specific terms inside of packages by using a combination of ?? and ::. The double question marks indicate a search for a specific term. In the example above, we are searching for occurrences of the term "delim" in all base functions, using the double colon. R also allows you to perform less structured help searches with help.search and RSiteSearch. The help.search function will search all help files in your installed packages for some term, which in the above example is "delimited." Alternatively, you can search the R website, which includes help files and the mailing lists archive, using the RSiteSearch function. Please note, this chapter is by no means meant to be an exhaustive review of R or the functions used in this section. As such, we *highly recommend* using these search functions to explore R's base functions on your own.

For the UFO data there are several parameters in read.delim that we will need to set by hand in order to properly read in the data. First, we need to tell the function how the data are delimited. We know this is a tab-delimited file, so we set sep to the tab character. Next, when read.delim is reading in data it attempts to convert each column of data into an R data type using several heuristics. In our case, all of the columns are strings, but the default setting for all read.* functions is to convert strings to factor types. This class is meant for categorical variables, but we do not want this. As such, we have to set stringsAsFactors=FALSE to prevent this. In fact, it is always a good practice to switch off this default, especially when working with unfamiliar data.

The term "categorical variable" refers to a type of data that denotes an observation's membership in a category. In statistics categorical variables are very important because we may be interested in what makes certain observations belong to a certain type. In R we represent categorical variables as factor types, which essentially assigns numeric references to string labels. In this case, we convert certain strings—such as state abbreviations—into categorical variables using as.factor, which assigns a unique numeric ID to each state abbreviation in the data set. We will repeat this process many times.

Also, this data does not include a column header as its first row, so we will need to switch off that default as well to force R to not use the first row in the data as a header. Finally, there are many empty elements in the data, and we want to set those to the special R value NA. To do this we explicitly define the empty string as the na.string:

```
ufo<-read.delim("data/ufo/ufo_awesome.tsv", sep="\t", stringsAsFactors=FALSE,
    header=FALSE, na.strings="")
```

We now have a data frame containing all of the UFO data! Whenever working with data frames, especially if they are from external data sources, it is always a good idea to inspect the data by hand. Two great functions for doing this are head and tail. These functions will print the first and last six entries in a data frame:

```
head(ufo)
        V1       V2                        V3   V4     V5   V6
1 19951009 19951009           Iowa City, IA <NA>   <NA>  Man repts. witnessing "flash...
2 19951010 19951011           Milwaukee, WI <NA> 2 min.  Man  on Hwy 43 SW of Milwauk...
3 19950101 19950103             Shelton, WA <NA>   <NA>  Telephoned Report:CA woman v...
4 19950510 19950510            Columbia, MO <NA> 2 min.  Man repts. son's bizarre sig...
5 19950611 19950614             Seattle, WA <NA>   <NA>  Anonymous caller repts. sigh...
6 19951025 19951024 Brunswick County, ND <NA> 30 min.  Sheriff's office calls to re...
```

The first obvious issue with the data frame is that the column names are generic. Using the documentation for this data set as a reference, we can assign more meaningful labels to the columns. Having meaningful column names for data frames is an important best practice. It makes your code and output easier to understand, both for you and other audiences. We will use the names function, which can either access the column labels for a data structure or assign them. From the data documentation, we construct a character vector the corresponds to the appropriate column names and pass it to the names functions with the data frame as its only argument:

```
names(ufo)<-c("DateOccurred","DateReported","Location","ShortDescription",
    "Duration","LongDescription")
```

From the head output and the documentation used to create column headings, we know that the first two columns of data are dates. As in other languages, R treats dates as a special type, and we will want to convert the date strings to actual date types. To do this we will use the as.Date function, which will take the date string and attempt to convert it to as Date object. With this data the strings have an uncommon date format of the form *YYYYMMDD*. As such, we will also have to specify a format string in as.Date so the function knows how to convert the strings. We begin by converting the DateOccurred column:

```
ufo$DateOccurred<-as.Date(ufo$DateOccurred, format="%Y%m%d")
Error in strptime(x, format, tz = "GMT") : input string is too long
```

We've just come upon our first error! Though a bit cryptic, the error message contains the substring "input string too long", which indicates that some of the entries in the DateOccurred column are too long to match the format string we provided. Why might this be the case? We are dealing with a large text file, so perhaps some of the data was malformed in the original set. Assuming this is the case, those data points will not be parsed correctly when being loaded by read.delim and that would cause this sort of error. Because we are dealing with real world data, we'll need to do some cleaning by hand.

Converting date strings, and dealing with malformed data

To address this problem we first need to locate the rows with defective date strings, then decide what to do with them. We are fortunate in this case because we know from the error that the errant entries are "too long." Properly parsed strings will always be eight characters long, i.e., "YYYYMMDD". To find the problem rows, therefore, we simply need to find those that have strings with more than eight characters. As a best practice, we first inspect the data to see what the malformed data looks like, in order to get a better understanding of what has gone wrong. In this case, we will use the head function, as before, to examine the data returned by our logical statement.

Later, to remove these errant rows we will use the ifelse function to construct a vector of TRUE and FALSE values to identify the entries that are eight characters long (TRUE) and those that are not (FALSE). This function is a vectorized version of the typical if-else logical switch for some Boolean test. We will see many examples of vectorized operations in R. They are the preferred mechanism for iterating over data because they are often—but not always—more efficient:[*]

```
head(ufo[which(nchar(ufo$DateOccurred)!=8 | nchar(ufo$DateReported)!=8),1])
[1] "ler@gnv.ifas.ufl.edu"
[2] "0000"
[3] "Callers report sighting a number of soft white balls of lights headingin
an easterly directing then changing direction to the west beforespeeding off to
the north west."
[4] "0000"
[5] "0000"
[6] "0000"

good.rows<-ifelse(nchar(ufo$DateOccurred)>!=8 | nchar(ufo$DateReported)!=8,
FALSE,TRUE)
length(which(!good.rows))
[1] 371
ufo<-ufo[good.rows,]
```

We use several useful R functions to perform this search. We need to know the length of the string in each entry of DateOccurred and DateReported, so we use the nchar function to compute this. If that length is not equal to eight, then we return FALSE. Once we have the vectors of Booleans, we want to see how many entries in the data frame have been malformed. To do this, we use the which command to return a vector of vector indices that are FALSE. Next, we compute the length of that vector to find the number of bad entries. With only 371 rows not conforming, the best option is to simply remove these entries and ignore them. At first, we might worry that losing 371 rows of data is a bad idea, but there are over sixty-thousand total rows, so we will simply ignore those rows and continue with the conversion to Date types:

```
ufo$DateOccurred<-as.Date(ufo$DateOccurred, format="%Y%m%d")
ufo$DateReported<-as.Date(ufo$DateReported, format="%Y%m%d")
```

Next we will need to clean and organize the location data. Recall from the previous head call that the entries for UFO sightings in the United States take the form "City, State". We can use R's regular expression integration to split these strings into separate columns and identify those entries that do not conform. The latter portion (identifying those that do not conform) is particularly important because we are only interested in sighting variation in the United States and will use this information to isolate those entries.

Organizing location data

To manipulate the data in this way, we will first construct a function that takes a string as input and performs the data cleaning. Then we will run this function over the location data using one of the vectorized apply functions:

[*] For a brief introduction to vectorized operations in R see [LF08].

```
get.location<-function(l) {
  split.location<-tryCatch(strsplit(l,",")[[1]], error= function(e) return(c(NA, NA)))
  clean.location<-gsub("^ ","",split.location)
  if (length(clean.location)>2) {
    return(c(NA,NA))
  }
  else {
    return(clean.location)
  }
}
```

There are several subtle things happening in this function. First, notice that we are wrapping the strsplit command in R's error handling function, tryCatch. Again, not all of the entries are of the proper "City, State" form, and in fact some do not even contain a comma. The strsplit function will throw an error if the split character is not matched, therefore, we have to catch this error. In our case, when there is no comma to split we will return a vector of NA to indicate that this entry is not valid. Next, the original data included leading whitespace, so we will use the gsub function (part of R's suite of functions for working with regular expressions) to remove the leading white-space from each character. Finally, we add an additional check to ensure that only the location vectors of length two are returned. Many non-U.S. entries have multiple commas, creating larger vectors from the strsplit function. In this case, we will again return an NA vector.

With the function defined, we will use the lapply function, short for "list-apply," to iterate this function over all strings in the Location column. As mentioned, the apply family of functions in R are extremely useful. They are constructed of the form apply(vector, function), and return results of the vectorized application of the function to the vector in a specific form. In our case, we are using lapply, which always returns a list:

```
city.state<-lapply(ufo$Location, get.location)
head(city.state)
[[1]]
[1] "Iowa City" "IA"

[[2]]
[1] "Milwaukee" "WI"

[[3]]
[1] "Shelton" "WA"

[[4]]
[1] "Columbia" "MO"

[[5]]
[1] "Seattle" "WA"

[[6]]
[1] "Brunswick County" "ND"
```

From above, a `list` in R is a key-value style data structures, wherein the keys are indexed by the double-bracket and values by the single bracket. In our case the keys are simply integers, but `lists` can also have strings as keys.† Though convenient, having the data stored in a `list` is not desirable, as we would like to add the city and state information to the data frame as separate columns. To do this we will need to convert this long list into a two-column matrix, with the city data as the leading column:

```
location.matrix<-do.call(rbind, city.state)
ufo<-transform(ufo, USCity=location.matrix[,1], USState=tolower(location.matrix[,2]),
    stringsAsFactors=FALSE)
```

To construct a matrix from the `list`, we use the `do.call` function. Similar to the `apply` functions, `do.call` executes a function call over a list. We will often use the combination of `lapply` and `do.call` to manipulate data. Above we pass the `rbind` function, which will "row-bind" all of the vectors in the `city.state` list to create a matrix. To get this into the data frame we use the `transform` function. We create two new columns; `USCity` and `USState`, from the first and second columns of `location.matrix`, respectively. Finally, the state abbreviations are inconsistent, with some uppercase and others lowercase, so we use the `tolower` function to make them all lowercase.

Dealing with data outside our scope

The final issue related to data cleaning we must consider concerns entries that meet the "City, State" form, but are not from the U.S. Specifically, the data include several UFO sightings from Canada, which also take this form. Fortunately, none of the Canadian province abbreviations match U.S. state abbreviations. We can use this information to identify non-U.S. entries by constructing a vector of U.S. state abbreviations and only keeping those entries in the `USState` column that match an entry in this vector:

```
us.states<-c("ak","al","ar","az","ca","co","ct","de","fl","ga","hi","ia","id","il",
    "in","ks","ky","la","ma","md","me","mi","mn","mo","ms","mt","nc","nd","ne","nh",
    "nj","nm","nv","ny","oh","ok","or","pa","ri","sc","sd","tn","tx","ut","va","vt",
    "wa","wi","wv","wy")
ufo$USState<-us.states[match(ufo$USState,us.states)]
ufo$USCity[is.na(ufo$USState)]<-NA
```

To find the entries in the `USState` column that do not match a U.S. state abbreviation, we use the `match` function. This function takes two arguments: the first are the values to be matched, and the second those to be matched against. What is returned is a vector of the same length as the first argument, in which the values are the index of entries in that vector that match some value in the second vector. If no match is found, the function returns `NA` by default. In our case, we are only interested in which entries are `NA`, as these are those entries that do not match a state. We then use the `is.na` function to find which entries are not U.S. states and reset them to `NA` in the `USState` column. Finally, we also set those indices in the `USCity` column to `NA` for consistency.

---

† For a thorough introduction to `lists`, see Chapter 1 of [Spe08].

Our original data frame now has been manipulated to the point that we can extract from it only the data we are interested in. Specifically, we want a subset that includes only U.S. incidents of UFO sightings. By replacing entries that did not meet this criteria in the previous steps, we can use the subset command to create a new data frame of only U.S. incidents:

```
ufo.us<-subset(ufo, !is.na(USState))
head(ufo.us)
  DateOccurred DateReported                Location ShortDescription Duration
1   1995-10-09   1995-10-09      Iowa City, IA                  <NA>     <NA>
2   1995-10-10   1995-10-11      Milwaukee, WI                  <NA>   2 min.
3   1995-01-01   1995-01-03        Shelton, WA                  <NA>     <NA>
4   1995-05-10   1995-05-10       Columbia, MO                  <NA>   2 min.
5   1995-06-11   1995-06-14        Seattle, WA                  <NA>     <NA>
6   1995-10-25   1995-10-24 Brunswick County, ND                  <NA>  30 min.

                LongDescription           USCity    USState
1 Man repts. witnessing "flash...      Iowa City    ia
2 Man  on Hwy 43 SW of Milwauk...      Milwaukee    wi
3 Telephoned Report:CA woman v...        Shelton    wa
4 Man repts. son's bizarre sig...       Columbia    mo
5 Anonymous caller repts. sigh...        Seattle    wa
6 Sheriff's office calls to re...   Brunswick County    nd
```

Aggregating and organizing the data

We now have our data in a format in which we can begin analyzing it! In the previous section we spent a lot of time getting the data properly formatted and identifying the relevant entries for our analysis. In this section we will explore the data to further narrow our focus. These data have two primary dimensions: space (where the sighting happened) and time (when a sighting occurred). We focused on the former in the previous section, but here we will focus on the latter. First, we use the summary function on the DateOccurred column to get a sense of this chronological range of the data:

```
summary(ufo.us$DateOccurred)
     Min.      1st Qu.      Median         Mean      3rd Qu.         Max.
"1400-06-30" "1999-09-06" "2004-01-10" "2001-02-13" "2007-07-26" "2010-08-30"
```

Surprisingly, this data goes back quite a long time:the oldest UFO sighting comes from 1400! Given this outlier, the next question is: how are these data distributed over time? And is it worth analyzing the entire time series? A quick way to look at this visually is to construct a histogram. We will discuss histograms in more detail in the next chapter, but for now you should know that histograms allow you to bin your data by a given dimension and observe the frequency with which your data falls into those bins. The dimension of interest here is time, so we construct a histogram that bins the data over time:

```
quick.hist<-ggplot(ufo.us, aes(x=DateOccurred))+geom_histogram()+
    scale_x_date(major="50 years")
ggsave(plot=quick.hist, filename="../images/quick_hist.png", height=6, width=8)
stat_bin: binwidth defaulted to range/30. Use 'binwidth = x' to adjust this.
```

There are several things to note here. This is our first use of the ggplot2 package, which we will use throughout the book for all of our data visualizations. In this case, we are constructing a very simple histogram, which we only requires a single line of code. First, we create a ggplot object and pass it the UFO data frame as its initial argument. Next, we set the x-axis aesthetic to the DateOccurred column, as this is the frequency we are interested in examining. With ggplot2 we must always work with data frames, and the first argument to create a ggplot object must always be a data frame. ggplot2 is an R implementation of Leland Wilkinson's *Grammar of Graphics* [Wil05]. This means the package adheres to this particular philosophy for data visualization, and all visualizations will be built up as a series of layers. For this histogram, the initial layer is the x-axis data, namely the UFO sighting dates. Next, we add an histogram layer with the geom_histogram function. In this case, we will use the default settings for this function, but, as we will see later, this default is often not a good choice. Finally, because this data spans such a long time period, we will rescale the x-axis labels to occur every 50 years with the scale_x_date function.

Once the ggplot object has been constructed, we use the ggsave function to output the visualization to a file. We could have also used > print(quick.hist) to print the visualization to the screen. Note the warning message that is printed when you draw the visualization. There are many ways to bin data in a histogram, and we will discuss this in detail the next chapter, but this warning is provided to let you know exactly how ggplot2 does the binning by default.

We are now ready to explore the data with this visualization, which is illustrated in Figure 1-5.

The results of this analysis are stark. The vast majority of the data occur between 1960 and 2010, with the majority of UFO sightings occurring within the last two decades. For our purposes, therefore, we will focus on only those sightings that occurred between 1990 and 2010. This will allow us to exclude the outliers and compare relatively comparable units during the analysis. As before, we will used the subset function to create a new data frame that meets this criteria:

```
ufo.us<-subset(ufo.us, DateOccurred>=as.Date("1990-01-01"))
nrow(ufo.us)
[1] 46347
```

While this removes many more entries than we eliminated while cleaning the data, it still leaves us with over forty-six thousand observations to analyze. Next, we must begin organizing the data such that it can be used to address our central question: what, if any, seasonal variation exists for UFO sightings in U.S. states? To address this, we must first ask: what do we mean by "seasonal?" There are many ways to aggregate time series data with respect to seasons; by week, month, quarter, year, etc. But which way of

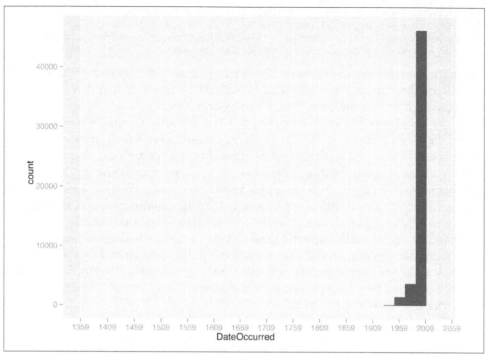

Figure 1-5. Exploratory histogram of UFO data over time

aggregating our data is most appropriate here? The `DateOccurred` column provides UFO sighting information by the day, but there is considerable inconsistency in terms of the coverage throughout the entire set. We need to aggregate the data in a way that puts the amount of data for each state on relatively level planes. In this case, doing so by year-month is the best option. This aggregation also best addresses the core of our question, as monthly aggregation will give good insight into seasonal variations.

We need to count the number of UFO sightings that occurred in each state by all year-month combinations from 1990-2010. First, we will need to create a new column in the data that corresponds to the year and months present in the data. We will use the `strftime` function to convert the `Date` objects to a string of the "YYYY-MM" format. As before, we will set the `format` parameter accordingly to get the strings:

```
ufo.us$YearMonth<-strftime(ufo.us$DateOccurred, format="%Y-%m")
```

Notice that in this case we did not use the `transform` function to add a new column to the data frame. Rather, we simply referenced a column name that did not exists and R automatically added it. Both methods for adding new columns to a data frame are useful, and we will switch between them depending on the particular task. Next, we want to count the number of times each state and year-month combination occurs in the data. For the first time we will use the `ddply` function, which is part of the extremely useful `plyr` library for manipulating data.

The plyr family of functions work a bit like the map-reduce style data aggregation tools that have risen in popularity over the past several years. They attempt to group data in some specific way meaningful to all observations, and then do some calculation on each of these group and return the results. For this task we want to group the data by state abbreviations and the year-month column we just created. Once the data is grouped as such, we count the number of entries in each group and return that as a new column. Here we will simply use the nrow function to reduce the data by the number of rows in each group:

```
sightings.counts<-ddply(ufo.us,.(USState,YearMonth), nrow)
head(sightings.counts)
USState YearMonth V1
1       ak  1990-01  1
2       ak  1990-03  1
3       ak  1990-05  1
4       ak  1993-11  1
5       ak  1994-11  1
6       ak  1995-01  1
```

We now have the number of UFO sightings for each state by the year and month. From the head call above, however, we can see that there may be a problem with using the data as is, because it contains a lot of missing values. For example, we see that there was one UFO sighting in January, March, and May of 1990 in Arkansas; but no entries appear for February or April. Presumably, there were no UFO sightings in these months, but the data does not include entries for non-sightings, so we have to go back and add these as zeroes.

We need a vector of years and months that span the entire data set. From this we can check to see if they are already in the data, and if not, add them as zeroes. To do this, we will create a sequence of dates using the seq.Date function, and then format them to match the data in our data frame:

```
date.range<-seq.Date(from=as.Date(min(ufo.us$DateOccurred)),
    to=as.Date(max(ufo.us$DateOccurred)), by="month")
date.strings<-strftime(date.range, "%Y-%m")
```

With the new date.strings vector, we need to create a new data frame that has all year-months and states. We will use this to performing the matching with the UFO sighting data. As before, we will use the lapply function to create the columns and the do.call function to convert this to a matrix and then data frame:

```
states.dates<-lapply(us.states,function(s) cbind(s,date.strings))
states.dates<-data.frame(do.call(rbind, states.dates), stringsAsFactors=FALSE)
head(states.dates)
s date.strings
1 ak       1990-01
2 ak       1990-02
3 ak       1990-03
4 ak       1990-04
5 ak       1990-05
6 ak       1990-06
```

The states.dates data frame now contains entries for every year, month and state combination possible in the data. Note that there are now entries for February and April 1990 for Arkansas. To add in the missing zeroes to the UFO sighting data, we need to merge this data with our original data frame. To do this, we will use the merge function, which takes two ordered data frames and attempts to merge them by common columns. In our case, we have two data frames ordered alphabetically by U.S. state abbreviations and chronologically by year and month. We need to tell the function which columns to merge these data frames by. We will set the by.x and by.y parameters according to the matching column names in each data frame. Finally, we set the all parameter to TRUE, which instructs the function to include entries that do not match and fill them with NA. Those entries in the V1 column will be those state, year, and month entries for which no UFOs were sighted:

```
all.sightings<-merge(states.dates,sightings.counts,by.x=c("s","date.strings"),
    by.y=c("USState","YearMonth"),all=TRUE)
head(all.sightings)
  s date.strings V1
1 ak       1990-01  1
2 ak       1990-02 NA
3 ak       1990-03  1
4 ak       1990-04 NA
5 ak       1990-05  1
6 ak       1990-06 NA
```

The final steps for data aggregation are simple housekeeping. First, we will set the column names in the new all.sightings data frame to something meaningful. This is done in exactly the same way as we did it at the outset. Next, we will convert the NA entries to zeroes using the is.na function, again. Finally, we will convert the Year Month and State columns to the appropriate types. Using the date.range vector we created in the previous step and the rep function to create a new vector that repeats a given vector, we replace the year and month strings with the appropriate Date object. Again, it is better to keep dates as Date objects rather than strings because we can compare Date objects mathematically, but we can't do that easily with strings. Likewise, the state abbreviations are better represented as a categorical variables than strings, so we convert these to factor types. We will describe factors, and other R data types, in more detail in the next chapter:

```
names(all.sightings)<-c("State","YearMonth","Sightings")
all.sightings$Sightings[is.na(all.sightings$Sightings)]<-0
all.sightings$YearMonth<-as.Date(rep(date.range,length(us.states)))
all.sightings$State<-as.factor(toupper(all.sightings$State))
```

We are now ready to analyze the data visually!

Analyzing the data

For this data we will only address the core question by analyzing it visually. For the remainder of the book we will combine both numeric and visual analyses, but as this example is only meant to introduce core R programming paradigms, we will stop at the visual component. Unlike the previous histogram visualization, however, we will take greater care with ggplot2 to build the visual layers explicitly. This will allow us to create a visualization that directly addresses the question of seasonal variation among states overtime and produce a more professional-looking visualization.

We will construct the visualization all at once below, then explain each layer individually:

```
state.plot<-ggplot(all.sightings, aes(x=YearMonth,y=Sightings))
+geom_line(aes(color="darkblue"))+
    facet_wrap(~State,nrow=10,ncol=5)+
    theme_bw()+
    scale_color_manual(values=c("darkblue"="darkblue"),legend=FALSE)+
    scale_x_date(major="5 years", format="%Y")+
    xlab("Time")+ylab("Number of Sightings")+
    opts(title="Number of UFO sightings by Month-Year and U.S. State (1990-2010)")
ggsave(plot=state.plot, filename="../images/ufo_sightings.pdf",width=14,height=8.5)
```

As always, the first step is to create a ggplot object with a data frame as its first argument. Here, we are using the all.sightings data frame we created in the previous step. Again, we need to build an aesthetic layer of data to plot, and in this case the x-axis is the YearMonth column and the y-axis is the Sightings data. Next, to show seasonal variation among states, we will plot a line for each state. This will allow us to observe any spikes, lulls, or oscillation in the number of UFO sightings for each state over time. To do this, we will use the geom_line function and set the color to "darkblue" to make the visualization easier to read.

As we have seen throughout this case, the UFO data is fairly rich and includes many sightings across the United States over a long period of time. Knowing this, we need to think of a way to break up this visualization such that we can observe the data for each state, but also compare it to the others. If we plot all of the data in a single panel it will be very difficult to discern variation. To check this, run the first line of code from the above block, but replace color="darkblue" with color=State and enter > print(state.plot) at the console. A better approach would be to plot the data for each state individually, and order them in a grid for easy comparison.

To create a multi-faceted plot, we use the facet_wrap function and specify that the panels be created by the State variable, which is already a factor type, i.e., categorical. We also explicitly define the number of rows and columns in the grid, which is easier in our case because we know we are creating 50 different plots.

The ggplot2 package has many plotting themes. The default theme is the one we used in the first example and has a grey background with dark grey gridlines. While it is strictly a matter of taste, we prefer using a white background for this plot, since that will make it easier to see slight difference among data points in our visualization. We add the theme_bw layer, which will produce a plot with a white background and black gridlines. Once you become more comfortable with ggplot2, we recommend experimenting with different defaults to find the one you prefer.‡

The remaining layers are done as housekeeping to make sure the visualization has a professional look and feel. Though not formally required, paying attention to these details is what can separate amateurish plots from professional-looking data visualizations. The scale_color_manual function is used to specify that the string "darkblue" corresponds to the web-safe color "darkblue." While this may seem repetitive, it is at the core of ggplot2's design, which requires explicit definition of details, such as color. In fact, ggplot2 tends to think of colors as a way of distinguishing among different types or categories of data; and, as such, prefers to have a factor type used to specify color. In our case we are defining a color explicitly using a string and therefore have to define the value of that string with the scale_color_manual function.

As we did before, we use the scale_x_date to specify the major gridlines in the visualization. Since this data spans twenty years, we will set these to be at regular five year intervals. Then we set the tick labels to be the year in a full four digit format. Next, we set the x-axis label to "Time" and the y-axis label to "Number of Sightings" by using the xlab and ylab functions respectively. Finally, we use the opts function to give the plot a title. There are many more options available in the opts function, and in later chapters we will see some of them, but there are many more beyond the scope of this book.

With all of the layers built, we are now ready to render the image with ggsave and analyze the data. The results are shown in Figure 1-6.

There are many interesting observations that arise in this analysis. We see that California and Washington are large outliers in terms of the number of UFO sightings reported in these states compared to the others. Between these outliers there are also interesting differences. In California, the number of UFO sightings seems to be somewhat random over time, but steadily increasing since 1995; while in Washington, the seasonal variation seems to be very consistent over time, with regular peaks and valleys in UFO sightings starting from about 1995.

‡ For more information on ggplot2 themes, see Chapter 8 of [Wic09].

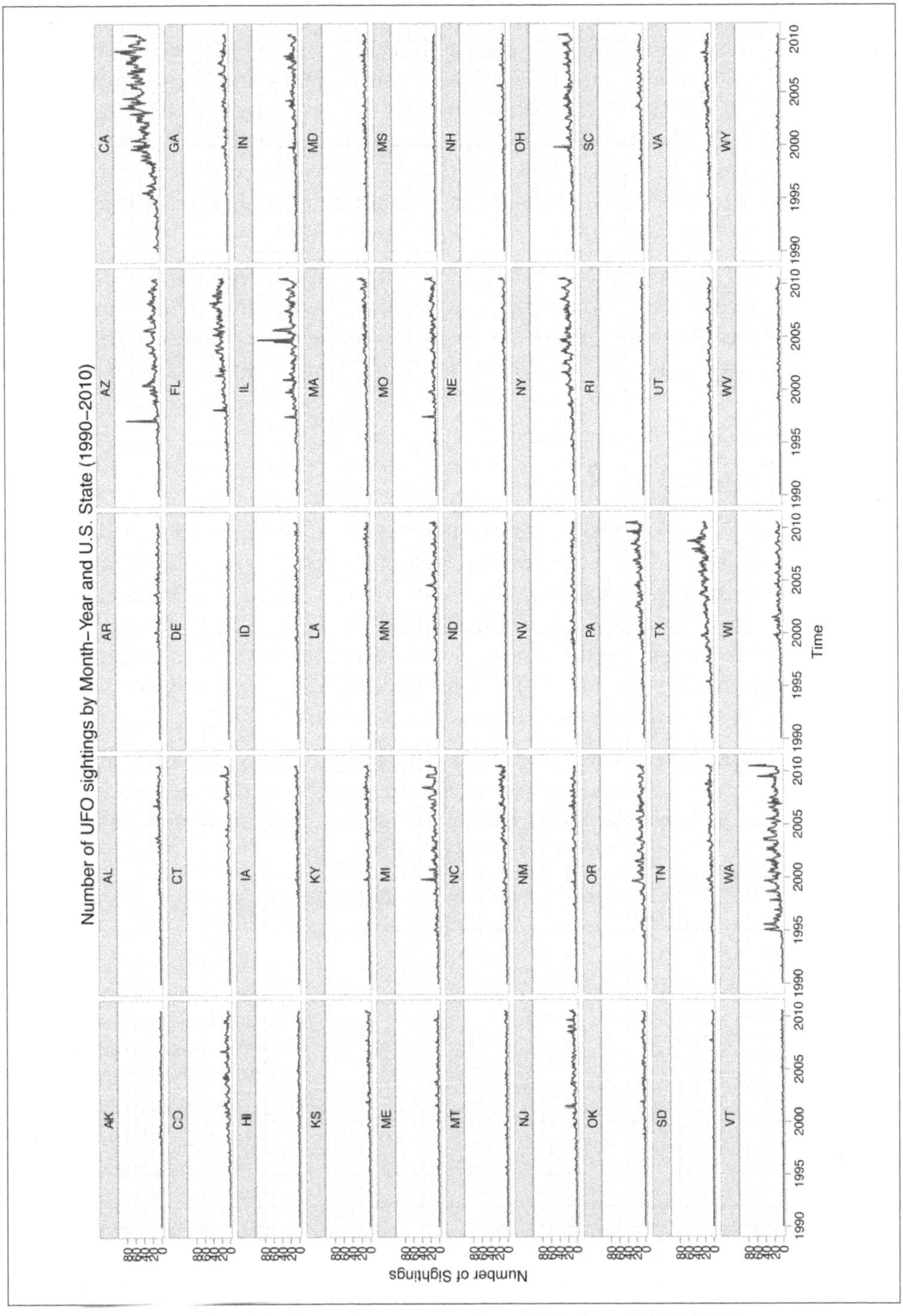

Figure 1-6. Number of UFO sightings by Year-Month and U.S. State (1990-2010)

We can also notice that many states experience sudden spikes in the number of UFO sightings reported. For example, Arizona, Florida, Illinois, and Montana seem to have experienced spikes around mid-1997, while Michigan, Ohio, and Oregon experienced similar spikes in late 1999. Only Michigan and Ohio are geographically close among these groups. If we do not believe that these are actually the result of extraterrestrial visitors, what are some alternative explanations? Perhaps there was increased vigilance among citizens to look to the sky as the millennium came to a close, causing heavier reporting of false sightings.

If, however, you are sympathetic to the notion that we may be regularly hosting visitors from outer space, there is also evidence to pique your curiosity. In fact, there is surprising regularity of these sightings in many states in the United States, with evidence of regional clustering as well. It is almost as if the sightings really contain a meaningful pattern.

Further Reading on R

This introductory case is by no means meant to be an exhaustive review of the language. Rather, we used this data set to introduce several R paradigms related to loading, cleaning, organizing, and analyzing data. We will revisit many of the functions and processes reviewed above in the following chapters, along with many others. For those readers interested in gaining more practice and familiarity with R before proceeding, there are many excellent resources. These resources can roughly be divided into either reference books and texts or online resources, as shown in Table 1-3.

In the next chapter, we will review exploratory data analysis. Much of the above case study involved exploring data, but we moved through these steps rather quickly. In the next section we will consider the process of data exploration much more deliberately.

Table 1-3. R references

Title	Author	Reference	Description
Text References			
Data Manipulation with R	Phil Spector	[Spe08]	A deeper review of many of the data manipulation topics covered in the previous section, and introduction to several techniques not covered.
R in a Nutshell	Joseph Adler	[Adl10]	A detailed exploration of all of R's base functions. This book takes the R manual and adds several practical examples.
Introduction to Scientific Programming and Simulation Using R	Owen Jones, Robert Maillardet, and Andrew Robinson	[JMR09]	Unlike other introductory texts to R, this book focuses on the primacy of learning the language first, then creating simulations.

Title	Author	Reference	Description
Data Analysis Using Regression and Multilevel/ Hierarchical Models	Andrew Gelman and Jennifer Hill	[GH06]	This text is heavily focused on doing statistical analyses, but all of the examples are in R and is an excellent resources for both learning the language and methods.
ggplot2: Elegant Graphics for Data Analysis	Hadley Wickham	[Wic09]	The definitive guide to creating data visualizations with ggplot2.

Online References

Title	Author	Reference	Description
An Introduction to R	Bill Venables and David Smith	http://lib.stat.cmu.edu/S/ Spoetry/Tutor/R_inferno.pdf (*http://cran.r-project.org/doc/ manuals/R-intro.html*)	An extensive and ever-changing introduction to the language from the R Core team.
The R Inferno	Patrick Burns	http://cran.r-project.org/doc/ manuals/R-intro.html (*http:// lib.stat.cmu.edu/S/Spoetry/Tu tor/R_inferno.pdf*)	An excellent introduction to R for the experienced programmer. The abstract says it best, "If you are using R and you think you're in hell, this is a map for you."
R for Programmers	Norman Matloff	*http://heather.cs.ucdavis.edu/ ~matloff/R/RProg.pdf*	Similar to the "R Inferno," this introduction is geared for programmers with experience in other languages.
The split-apply-combine strategy for data analysis	Hadley Wickham	*http://had.co.nz/plyr/plyr-intro -090510.pdf*	The author of plyr and provides an excellent introduction to the map-reduce paradigm in the context of his tools, with many examples.
R Data Analysis Examples	UCLA ATS	*http://www.ats.ucla.edu/stat/ r/dae/default.htm*	A great "Rosetta Stone" style introduction to those with experience in other statistical programming platforms, such as SAS, SPSS and Stata.

## CHAPTER 2

Data Exploration

Exploration vs. Confirmation

Whenever you work with data, it's helpful to imagine breaking up your analysis into two completely separate parts: exploration and confirmation. The distinction between exploratory data analysis and confirmatory data analysis comes down to us from the famous John Tukey,[*] who emphasized the importance of designing simple tools for practical data analysis. In Tukey's mind, the exploratory steps in data analysis involve using summary tables and basic visualizations to search for hidden patterns in your data. In this chapter, we'll describe some of the basic tools that R provides for summarizing your data numerically and then we'll teach you how to make sense of the results. After that, we'll show you some of the tools that exist in R for visualizing your data; at the same time, we'll give you a whirlwind tour of the basic visual patterns that you should keep an eye out for in any visualization.

But, before you start searching through your first data set, we should warn you about a real danger that's present whenever you explore data: you're likely to find patterns that aren't really there. The human mind is designed to find patterns in the world and will do so even when those patterns are just quirks of chance. You don't need a degree in statistics to know that we human beings will easily find shapes in clouds after looking at them for only a few seconds. And plenty of people have convinced themselves that they've discovered hidden messages in run-of-the-mill texts like Shakespeare's plays. Because we humans are vulnerable to discovering patterns that won't stand up to careful scrutiny, the exploratory step in data analysis can't exist in isolation: it needs to be accompanied by a confirmatory step. Think of confirmatory data analysis as a sort of mental hygiene routine that we use to clean off our beliefs about the world after we've gone slogging through the messy—and sometimes lawless—world of exploratory data visualization.

---

[*] The same person who invented the word "bit".

Confirmatory data analysis usually employs two methods:

1. Testing a formal model of the pattern that you think you've found on a new data set you didn't use to find the pattern
2. Using probability theory to test whether the patterns you've found in your original data set could reasonably have been produced by chance.

Because confirmatory data analysis requires more math than exploratory data analysis, this chapter is exclusively concerned with exploratory tools. In practice, that means that we'll focus on numeric summaries of your data and some standard visualization tools. The numerical summaries we'll describe are the stuff of introductory statistics courses: means, modes, percentiles, medians, standard deviations, and variances. The visualization tools we'll use are also some of the most basic tools that you would learn about in an "Intro to Stats" course: histograms, kernel density estimates, and scatter-plots. We think simple visualizations are often underappreciated and we hope we can convince you that you can often learn a lot about your data using only these basic tools. Much more sophisticated techniques will come up in the later chapters of this book, but the intuitions for analyzing data are best built up while working with the simplest of tools.

What is Data?

Before we start to describe some of the basic tools that you can use to explore your data, we should agree on what we mean when we use the word "data". It would be easy to write an entire book about the possible definitions of the word "data," because there are so many important questions you might want to ask about any so-called data set. For example, you often would want to know how the data you have was generated and whether the data can reasonably be expected to be representative of the population you truly want to study: while you could learn a lot about the social structure of the Amazonian Indians by studying records of their marriages, it's not clear that you'd learn something that applied very well to other cultures in the process. The interpretation of data requires that you know something about the source of your data: often the only way to separate causation from correlation is to know whether the data you're working with was generated experimentally or was only recorded observationally because experimental data wasn't available.

While these sorts of concerns are interesting issues that we hope you'll want to learn about some day,[†] we're going to completely avoid issues of data collection during this book. For our purposes, the subtler philosophical issues of data analysis are going to be treated as if they were perfectly separable from the sorts of prediction problems for which we're going to use machine learning techniques. In the interest of pragmatism, we're therefore going to use the following definition throughout the rest of this book:

---

† When you're interested, we'd recommend reading Judea Pearl's *Causality* [Pea05].

A "data set" is nothing more than a big table of numbers and strings in which every row describes a single observation of the real world and every column describes a single attribute that was measured for each of the observations represented by the rows. If you're at all familiar with databases, this definition of data should match your intuitions about the structure of database tables pretty closely. If you're worried that your data set isn't really a single table, let's just pretend that you've used R's merge, SQL's JOIN family of operations, or some of the other tools we described earlier to create a data set that looks like a single table.

We'll call this the "data as rectangles" model. While this viewpoint is clearly a substantial simplification, it will let us motivate many of the big ideas of data analysis visually, which we hope makes what are otherwise very abstract ideas a little more tangible. And the "data as rectangles" model serves another purpose: it lets us freely exploit ideas from database design as well as ideas from pure mathematics. If you're worried that you don't know much about matrices, don't worry: throughout this book you'll always be able to think of matrices as nothing more than two-dimensional arrays, i.e., a big table. As long as we assume we've working with rectangular arrays, we'll be able to use lots of powerful mathematical techniques without having to think very carefully about the actual mathematical operations being performed. For example, we won't explicitly use matrix multiplication anywhere in this book, even though almost every technique we're going to exploit can be described in terms of matrix multiplications, whether it's the standard linear regression model or the modern matrix factorization techniques that have become so popular lately thanks to the Netflix prize.

Because we'll treat data rectangles, tables, and matrices interchangeably, we ask for your patience when we switch back and forth between those terms throughout this book. Whatever term we use, you should just remember that we're thinking of something like Table 2-1 when we talk about data.

Table 2-1. Your authors

Name	Age
Drew Conway	28
John Myles White	29

Since data consists of rectangles, we can actually draw pictures of the sorts of operations we'll perform pretty easily. A numerical data summary involves reducing all of the rows from your table into a few numbers—often just a single number for each column in your data set. An example of this type of data summary is shown in Figure 2-1.

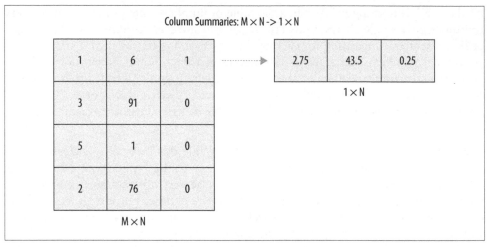

Figure 2-1. Summarizing many columns in one number per column

In contrast to a numerical summary, a visualization of a single column's contents usually involves reducing all of the rows from a single column in your data into one image.
An example of a visual summary of a single column is shown in Figure 2-2.

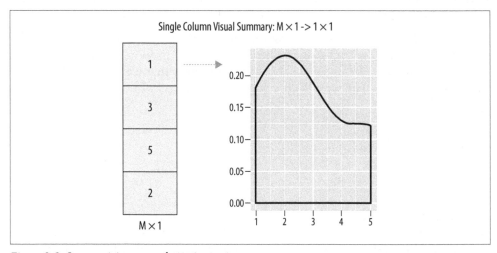

Figure 2-2. Summarizing one column in one image

Beyond the tools you can use for analyzing isolated columns, there are lots of tools you
can use to understand the relationships between multiple columns in your data set. For
example, computing the correlation between two columns turns all of the rows from
two columns of your table into a single number that summarizes the strength of the
relationship between those two columns. An example of this is shown in Figure 2-3.

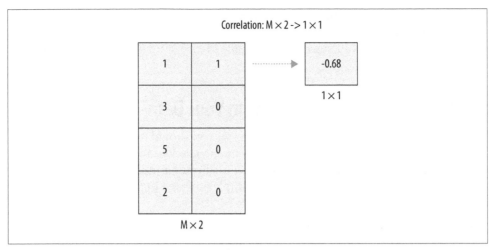

Figure 2-3. Correlation: summarizing two columns in one number

And there are other tools that go further: beyond relating pairs of columns together, you might want to reduce the number of columns in your data set if you think there's a lot of redundancy. Replacing many columns in your data set with a few columns or even just one is called dimensionality reduction. An example of what dimensionality reduction techniques achieve is shown in Figure 2-4.

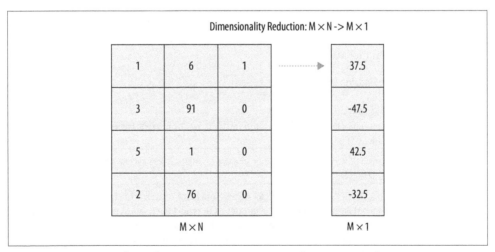

Figure 2-4. Dimensionality reduction: summarizing many columns in one column

As the pictures in Figures 2-1 to 2-4 suggest, summary statistics and dimensionality reduction move along opposite directions: summary statistics tell you something about how all of the rows in your data set behave when you move along a single column, while dimensionality reduction tools let you replace all of the columns in your data with a small number of columns that have a unique value for every row. When you're exploring data, both of these approaches can be helpful, because they allow you to turn the mountains of data you sometimes get handed into something that's immediately comprehensible.

Inferring the Types of Columns in Your Data

Before you do anything else with a new data set, you should try to find out what each column in your current table represents. Some people like to call this information a data dictionary, by which they mean that you might be handed a short verbal description of every column in the data set. For example, imagine that you had the unlabeled data set in Table 2-2 given to you.

Table 2-2. Unlabeled data

...	...	...
"1"	73.847017017515	241.893563180437
"0"	58.9107320370127	102.088326367840

Without any identifying information, it's really hard to know what to make of these numbers. Indeed, as a starting point you should figure out the type of each column: is the first column really a string, even though it looks like it contains only 0's and 1's? In the UFO example in the first chapter, we immediately labeled all of the columns of the data set we were given. When we're given a data set without labels, we can use some of the type determination functions built into R. Three of most important of these functions are shown in Table 2-3.

Table 2-3. Type determination in R

R function	Description
is.numeric	Returns TRUE if the entries of the vector are numbers, which can be either integers or floating points. Returns FALSE otherwise.
is.character	Returns TRUE if the entries of the vector are character strings. R does not provide a single character data type. Returns FALSE otherwise.
is.factor	Returns TRUE if the entries of the vector are levels of a factor, which is a data type used by R to represent categorical information (and FALSE otherwise). If you've used enumerations in SQL, a factor is somewhat analogous. It differs from a character vector in both its hidden internal representation and semantics: most statistical functions in R work on numeric vectors or factor vectors, but not on character vectors.

Having basic type information about each column can be very important as we move forward, because a single R function will often do different things depending of the type of its inputs. Those 0's and 1's stored as characters in our current data set need to be translated into numbers before we can use some of the built-in functions in R, but they actually need to be converted into factors if we're going to use some other built-in functions. In part, this tendency to move back and forth between types comes from a general tradition in machine learning for dealing with categorical distinctions. Many variables that really work like labels or categories are encoded mathematically as 0 and 1. You can think of these numbers as if they were Boolean values: 0 might indicate that an email is *not* spam, while a 1 might indicate that the email *is* spam. This specific use of 0's and 1's to describe qualitative properties of an object is often called dummy coding in machine learning and statistics. The dummy coding system should be distinguished from R's factors, which express qualitative properties using explicit labels.

 Factors in R can be thought of as labels, but the labels are actually encoded numerically in the background: when the programmer accesses the label, the numeric values are translated into the character labels specified in an indexed array of character strings. Because R uses a numeric coding in the background, naive attempts to convert the labels for an R factor into numbers will produce strange results, since you'll be given the actual encoding scheme's numbers rather than the numbers associated with the labels for the factor.

Tables 2-4 to 2-6 show the same data, but the data has been described with three different encoding schemes:

Table 2-4. Factor coding

MessageID	IsSpam
1	"Yes"
2	"No"

Table 2-5. Dummy coding

MessageID	IsSpam
1	1
2	0

Table 2-6. Physicists' coding

MessageID	IsSpam
1	1
2	-1

In the first table, IsSpam is meant to be treated directly as a factor in R, which is one way to express qualitative distinctions. In practice, it might be loaded as a factor or as a string depending on the data loading function you use: see the `stringsAsFactors` parameter that was described in "Loading libraries and the data" on page 12 for details.

With every new data set, you'll need to figure out whether the values are being loaded properly as factors or as strings after you've decided how you would like each column to be treated by R.

 If you are unsure, it is often better to begin by loading things as strings. You can always convert a string column to a factor column later.

In the second table, IsSpam is still a qualitative concept, but it's being encoded using numeric values that represent a Boolean distinction: 1 means IsSpam is true, while 0 means IsSpam is false. This style of numeric coding is actually required by some machine learning algorithms. For example, glm, the default function in R for using logistic regression, assumes that your variables are dummy coded.

Finally, in the third table, we show another type of numeric encoding for the same qualitative concept: in this encoding system, people use +1 and -1 instead of 1 and 0. This style of encoding qualitative distinctions is very popular with physicists, so you will eventually see it as you read more about machine learning. In this book, though, we'll completely avoid using this style of notation since we think it's a needless source of confusion to move back and forth between different ways of expressing the same distinctions.

Inferring Meaning

Even after you've figured out the type of each column, you may still not know what a column means. Determining what an unlabeled table of numbers describes can be surprisingly difficult. Let's return to the table that we showed earlier.

Table 2-7. Unlabeled data

...	...	...
"1"	73.847017017515	241.893563180437
"0"	58.9107320370127	102.088326367840

How much more sense does this table make if we tell you that (a) the rows describe individual people, (b) the first column is a dummy code indicating whether the person is male (written as a 1) or female (written as 0), (c) the second column is the person's height in inches and (d) the third column is the person's weight in pounds? The numbers suddenly have meaning when they're put into proper context and that will shape how you think about them.

But, sadly, you will sometimes not be given this sort of interpretative information. In those cases, human intuition, aided by liberally searching through Google, is often the only tool that we can suggest to you. Thankfully, your intuition can be substantially improved after you've looked at some numerical and visual summaries of the columns whose meaning you don't understand.

Numeric Summaries

One of the best ways to start making sense of a new data set is to compute simple numeric summaries of all of the columns. R is very well suited to doing this. If you've got just one column from a data set as a vector, summary will spit out the most obvious values you should look at first:

```
data.file <- file.path('data', '01_heights_weights_genders.csv')
heights.weights <- read.csv(data.file, header = TRUE, sep = ',')
heights <- with(heights.weights, Height)
summary(heights)

# Min. 1st Qu.  Median    Mean 3rd Qu.    Max.
#54.26   63.51   66.32   66.37   69.17   79.00
```

Asking for the summary of a vector of numbers from R will give you the numbers you saw above:

1. The minimum value in the vector.
2. The first quartile (which is also called the 25th percentile and is the smallest number that's bigger than 25% of your data).
3. The median (aka the 50th percentile).
4. The mean.
5. The 3rd quartile (aka the 75th percentile).
6. The maximum value.

This is close to everything you should ask for when you want a quick numeric summary of a data set. All that's really missing is the standard deviation of the column entries, a numeric summary we'll define later on in this chapter. In the following pages, we'll describe how to compute each of the numbers that summary produces separately and then we'll show you how to interpret them.

Means, Medians, and Modes

Learning to tell means and medians apart is one of the most tedious parts of the typical "Intro to Stats" class. It can take a little while to become familiar with those concepts, but we really do believe that you'll need to be able to tell them apart if you want to seriously work with data. In the interests of better pedagogy, we'll try to hammer home the meaning of those terms in two pretty different ways. First, we'll show you how to compute the mean and the median algorithmically. For most hackers, code is a more natural language to express ideas than mathematical symbols, so we think that rolling your own functions to compute means and medians will probably make more sense than showing you the defining equations for those two statistics. And later in this chapter, we'll show you how you can tell when the mean and median are different, by looking at the shape of your data in histograms and density plots.

Computing the mean is incredibly easy. In R, you would normally use the mean function. Of course, telling you to use a black-box function doesn't convey much of the intuition for what a mean is, so let's implement our own version of mean, which we'll call my.mean. It's just one line of R code, because the relevant concepts are already available as two other functions in R: sum and length.

```
my.mean <- function(x) {
  return(sum(x) / length(x))
}
```

That single line of code is all there is to a mean: you just add up all the numbers in your vector and then divide the sum by the length of the vector. As you'd expect, this function produces the average value of the numbers in your vector, x. The mean is so easy to compute in part because it doesn't have anything to do with the sorted positions of the numbers in your list.

The median is just the opposite: it entirely depends upon the relative position of the numbers in your list. In R, you would normally compute the median using median, but let's write our version, which we'll call my.median:

```
my.median <- function(x) {
  sorted.x <- sort(x)

  if (length(x) %% 2 == 0)
  {
    indices <- c(length(x) / 2, length(x) / 2 + 1)
    return(mean(sorted.x[indices]))
  }
  else
  {
    index <- ceiling(length(x) / 2)
    return(sorted.x[index])
  }
}
```

Just counting lines of code should tell you that the median takes a little bit more work to compute than the mean. As a first step, we had to sort the vector, because the median is essentially the number that's in the middle of your sorted vector. That's why the median is also called the 50th percentile or the 2nd quartile. Once you've sorted a vector, you can easily compute any of the other percentiles or quantiles just by splitting the list into two parts somewhere else along its length. To get the 25th percentile (also known as the 1st quartile), you can split the list at one quarter of its length.

The only problem with these informal definitions in terms of length is that they don't exactly make sense if your list has an even number of entries. When there's no single number that's exactly in the middle of your data set, you need to do some trickery to produce the median. The code we wrote above handles the even length vector case by taking the average of the two entries that would have been the median if only the list had contained an odd number of entries.

To make that point clear, here is a simple example in which the median has to be invented by averaging entries and another case in which the median is exactly equal to the middle entry of the vector:

```
my.vector <- c(0, 100)
my.vector
# [1]   0 100
mean(my.vector)
#[1] 50
median(my.vector)
#[1] 50
my.vector <- c(0, 0, 100)
mean(my.vector)
#[1] 33.33333
median(my.vector)
#[1] 0
```

Returning to our original heights and weights data set, let's compute the mean and median of the heights data. This will also give us an opportunity to test our code:

```
my.mean(heights)
#[1] 66.36756
my.median(heights)
#[1] 66.31807
mean(heights) - my.mean(heights)
#[1] 0
median(heights) - my.median(heights)
#[1] 0
```

The mean and median in this example are very close to each other. In a little bit, we'll explain why we should expect that to be the case given the shape of the data we're working with.

Since we've just described two of the three most prominent numbers from an intro stats course, you may be wondering why we haven't mentioned the mode. We'll talk about modes in a bit, but there's a reason we've ignored it so far: the mode, unlike the mean or median, doesn't always have a simple definition for the kinds of vectors we've been working with. Because it's not easy to automate, R doesn't have a built-in function that will produce the mode of a vector of numbers.

 The reason that it's complicated to define the mode of an arbitrary vector is that you need the numbers in the vector to repeat if you're going to define the mode numerically. When the numbers in a vector could be arbitrary floating point values, it's unlikely that any single numeric value would ever be repeated in the vector. For that reason, modes are only really defined visually for many kinds of data sets.

All that said, if you're still not sure about the math and are wondering what the mode should be in theory, it's supposed to be the number that occurs most often in your data set.

Quantiles

As we said just a moment ago, the median is the number that occurs at the 50% point in your data. To get a better sense of the range of your data, you might want to know what value is the lowest point in your data. That's the minimum value of your data set, which is computed using min in R:

```
min(heights)
#[1] 54.26313
```

And to get the highest/maximum point in your data set, you should use max in R:

```
max(heights)
#[1] 78.99874
```

Together, the min and max define the range of your data:

```
c(min(heights), max(heights))
#[1] 54.26313 78.99874
range(heights)
#[1] 54.26313 78.99874
```

Another way of thinking of these numbers is to think of the min as the number which 0% of your data is below and the max as the number which 100% of your data is below. Thinking that way leads to a natural extension: how can you find the number which N% of your data is below? The answer to that question is to use the quantile function in R. The Nth quantile is exactly the number which N% of your data is below.

By default, quantile will tell you the 0%, 25%, 50%, 75% and 100% points in your data:

```
quantile(heights)
#      0%      25%      50%      75%     100%
#54.26313 63.50562 66.31807 69.17426 78.99874
```

To get other locations, you can pass in the cut-offs you want as another argument to quantile called probs:

```
quantile(heights, probs = seq(0, 1, by = 0.20))
#      0%      20%      40%      60%      80%     100%
#54.26313 62.85901 65.19422 67.43537 69.81162 78.99874
```

Here we've used the seq function to produce a sequence of values between 0 and 1 that grows in 0.20 increments:

```
seq(0, 1, by = 0.20)
#[1] 0.0 0.2 0.4 0.6 0.8 1.0
```

Quantiles don't get emphasized as much in traditional statistics texts as means and medians, but they can be just as useful. If you run a customer service branch and keep records of how long it takes to respond to a customer's concerns, you might benefit a lot more from worrying about what happens to the first 99% of your customers than worrying about what happens to the median customer. And the mean customer might be even less informative if your data has a strange shape.

Standard Deviations and Variances

The mean and median of a list of numbers are both measures of something central: the median is literally in the center of list, while the mean is only effectively in the center once you've weighted all the items in the list by their values.

But central tendencies are only one thing you might want to know about your data. Equally important is to ask how far apart you expect the typical values to be, which we'll call the spread of your data. You can imagine defining the range of your data in a lot of ways. As we already said, you could use the definition that the range function implements: the range is defined by the min and max values. This definition misses two things we might want from a reasonable definition of spread:

1. The spread should only include most of the data, not all of it.
2. The spread shouldn't be completely determined by the two most extreme values in your data set, which are often outlier values that are not representative of your data set as a whole.

The min and max will match the outliers perfectly, which makes them fairly brittle definitions of spread. Another way to think about what's wrong with the min and max definition of range is to consider what happens if you change the rest of your data while leaving those two extreme values unchanged. In practice, you can move the rest of the data as much as you'd like inside those limits and still get the same min and max. In other words, the definition of range based on min and max effectively only depends on two of your data points, whether or not you have two data points or two million data points. Because you shouldn't trust any summary of your data that's insensitive to the vast majority of the points in the data, we'll move on to a better definition of the spread of a data set.

Now, there are a lot of ways you could try to meet the requirements we described above for a good numeric summary of data. For example, you could see what range contains 50% of your data and is centered around the median. In R, this is quite easy to do:

```
c(quantile(heights, probs = 0.25), quantile(heights, probs = 0.75))
```

Or you might want to be more inclusive and find a range that contains 95% of the data:

```
c(quantile(heights, probs = 0.025), quantile(heights, probs = 0.975))
```

These are actually really good measures of the spread of your data. When you work with more advanced statistical methods, these sorts of ranges will come up again and again. But, historically, statisticians have used a somewhat different measure of spread: specifically, they've used a definition called the variance. The idea is roughly to measure how far, on average, a given number in your data set is from the mean value. Rather than give a formal mathematical definition, let's define the variance computationally by writing our own variance function:

```
my.var <- function(x) {
  m <- mean(x)
  return(sum((x - m) ^ 2) / length(x))
}
```

As always, let's check that our implementation works by comparing it with R's **var**:

```
my.var(heights) - var(heights)
```

We're only doing a so-so job of matching R's implementation of **var**. In theory, there could be a few reasons for this, most of which are examples of how things can go wrong when you assume floating point arithmetic is perfectly accurate. But there's actually another reason that our code isn't working the same way that the built-in function does in R: the formal definition of variance doesn't divide out by the length of a vector, but rather by the length of the vector *minus one*. This is done because the variance that you can estimate from empirical data turns out, for fairly subtle reasons, to be biased downwards from its true value. To fix this for a data set with n points, you normally multiply your estimate of the variance by a scaling factor of n / (n - 1), which leads to an improved version of **my.var**:

```
my.var <- function(x) {
  m <- mean(x)
  return(sum((x - m) ^ 2) / (length(x) - 1))
}

my.var(heights) - var(heights)
```

With this second version of **my.var**, we match R's estimate of the variance perfectly. The floating point concerns we raised above could easily come up if had used longer vectors, but they didn't seem to matter with a data set of this size.

Now, the variance is a very natural measure of the spread of our data, but it's unfortunately much larger than almost any of the values in our data set. One obvious way to see this mismatch in scale is to look at the values that are one unit of variance away from the mean:

```
c(mean(heights) - var(heights), mean(heights) + var(heights))
#[1] 51.56409 81.17103
```

This range is actually larger than the range of the entire original data set:

```
c(mean(heights) - var(heights), mean(heights) + var(heights))
#[1] 51.56409 81.17103
range(heights)
#[1] 54.26313 78.99874
```

The reason we're so far out of bounds from our original data is that we defined variance by measuring the squared distance of each number in our list from the mean value, but we never undid that squaring step. To put everything back on the original scale, we need to replace the variance with the standard deviation, which is just the square root of the variance:

```
my.sd <- function(x) {
  return(sqrt(my.var(x)))
}
```

Before we do anything else, it's always good to check that your implementation makes sense relative to R's, which is called sd:

```
my.sd(heights) - sd(heights)
```

Since we're now computing values on the right scale, it'll be informative to recreate our estimate of the range of our data by looking at values that are one unit of standard deviation away from the mean:

```
c(mean(heights) - sd(heights), mean(heights) + sd(heights))
# [1] 62.52003 70.21509
range(heights)
#[1] 54.26313 78.99874
```

Now that we're using units of standard deviations instead of units of variances, we're solidly inside the range of our data. Still, it would be nice to get a sense of how tightly inside the data we are. One way to do this is to compare the standard deviation based range against a range defined using quantiles:

```
c(mean(heights) - sd(heights), mean(heights) + sd(heights))
# [1] 62.52003 70.21509

c(quantile(heights, probs = 0.25), quantile(heights, probs = 0.75))
#     25%      75%
#63.50562 69.17426
```

By using the quantile function, we can see that roughly 50% of our data is less than one standard deviation away from the mean. This is quite typical, especially for data with the shape that our heights data has. But to finally make that idea about the shape of our data precise, we need to start visualizing our data and define some formal terms for describing the shape of data.

Exploratory Data Visualization

Computing numerical summaries of your data is clearly valuable: it's the stuff of classical statistics after all. But, for many people, numbers don't convey the information they want to see very efficiently. Visualizing your data is often a more effective way to discover patterns in it. In this chapter, we'll cover the two simplest forms of exploratory data visualization: single column visualizations, which highlight the shape of your data, and two column visualizations, which highlight the relationship between pairs of columns. Beyond showing you the tools for visualizing your data, we'll also describe some of the canonical shapes you can expect to see when you start looking at data. These idealized shapes, also called distributions, are standard patterns that statisticians have studied over the years. When you find one of these shapes in your data, you can often make broad inferences about your data: how it originated, what sort of abstract properties it will have, and so on. Even when you think the shape you see is only a vague approximation to your data, the standard distributional shapes can provide you with building blocks that you can use to construct more complex shapes that match your data more closely.

All that said, let's get started by just visualizing the heights and weights data that we've been working with so far. It's actually a fairly complex data set that illustrates many of the ideas we'll come up against again and again throughout this book. The most typical single column visualization technique that people use is the histogram. In a histogram, you divide your data set into bins and then count the number of entries in your data that fall into each of the bins. For instance, we might use one inch bins to visualize our height data. We can do that in R as follows:

```
library('ggplot2')

data.file <- file.path('data', '01_heights_weights_genders.csv')

heights.weights <- read.csv(data.file, header = TRUE, sep = ',')

ggplot(heights.weights, aes(x = Height)) + geom_histogram(binwidth = 1)
```

Looking at Figure 2-5, something should jump out at you: there's a bell curve shape in your data. Most of the entries are in the middle of your data, near the mean and median height. But there's a danger that this shape is an illusion caused by the type of histogram we're using. One way to check this is to try using several other binwidths. This is something you should always keep in mind when working with histograms: the binwidths you use *impose* external structure on your data at the same time that they reveal *internal* structure in your data. The patterns you find, even when they're real, can go away very easily if you use the wrong settings for building a histogram:

```
ggplot(heights.weights, aes(x = Height)) + geom_histogram(binwidth = 5)
```

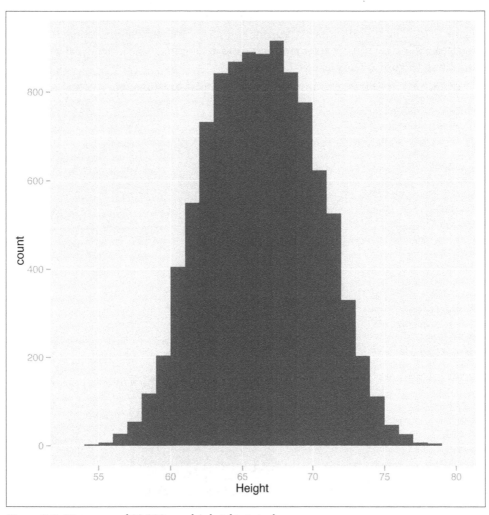

Figure 2-5. Histogram of 10,000 people's heights in inches

When we use too broad a binwidth, a lot of the structure in our data goes away (Figure 2-6). There's still a peak, but the symmetry we saw before seems to mostly disappear. This is called oversmoothing. And the opposite problem, called under-smoothing (Figure 2-7), is just as dangerous:

```
ggplot(heights.weights, aes(x = Height)) + geom_histogram(binwidth = 0.001)
```

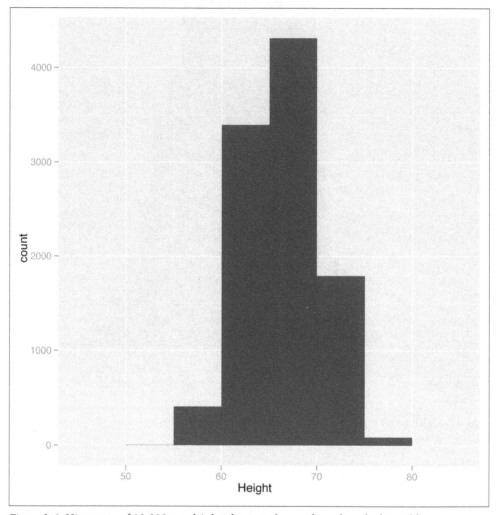

Figure 2-6. Histogram of 10,000 people's heights in inches, with too broad a binwidth

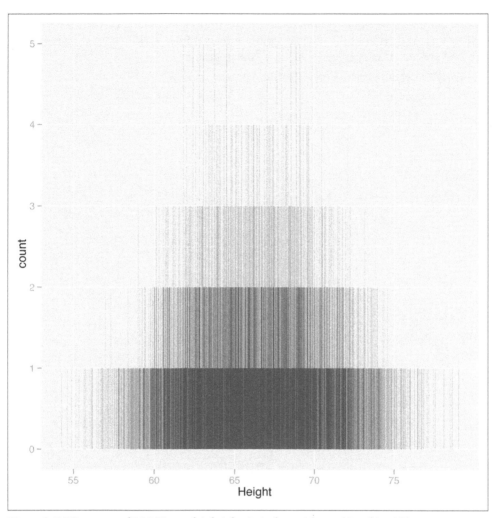

Figure 2-7. Histogram of 10,000 people's heights in inches, with too thin a binwidth

Here we've undersmoothed the data because we've used incredibly small bins. Because we have so much data, you can still learn something from this histogram, but a data set with 100 points would be basically worthless if you had used this sort of binwidth.

Because setting binwidths can be tedious and because even the best histogram is too jagged for our taste, we prefer an alternative to histograms called kernel density estimates (KDEs), or density plots. While density plots suffer from most of the same problems of oversmoothing and undersmoothing that plague histograms, we generally find them aesthetically superior—especially since density plots for large data sets look a more like the theoretical shapes we expect to find in our data. Additionally, density plots have some theoretical superiority over histograms: in theory, using a density plot should require fewer data points to reveal the underlying shape of your data than a histogram. And, thankfully, density plots (an example of which is shown in Figure 2-8) are just as easy to generate in R as histograms:

```
ggplot(heights.weights, aes(x = Height)) + geom_density()
```

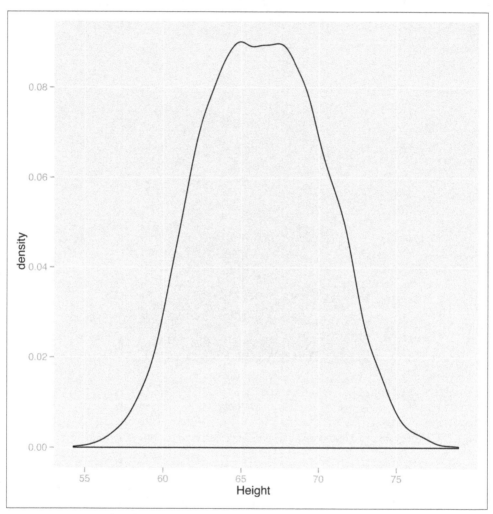

Figure 2-8. Density plot of 10,000 people's heights in inches

The smoothness of the density plot helps us discover the sorts of patterns that we personally find harder to see in histograms. Here, the density plot suggests that the data are suspiciously flat at the peak value. Since the standard bell curve shape we might expect to see isn't flat, this leads us to wonder if there might be more structure hidden in this data set. One thing you might try doing when you think there's some structure you're missing is to split up your plot by any qualitative variables you have available.

Here, we use the gender of each point to split up our data into two parts. Then we create a density plot in which there are two densities that get superimposed, but colored in differently to indicate the gender they represent. The resulting plot is shown in Figure 2-9:

```
ggplot(heights.weights, aes(x = Height, fill = Gender)) + geom_density()
```

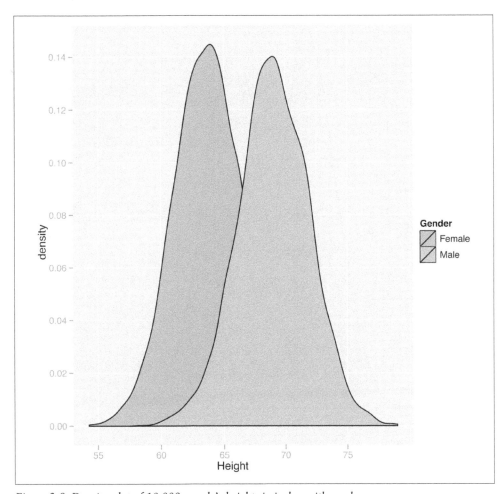

Figure 2-9. Density plot of 10,000 people's heights in inches with genders

In this plot, we suddenly see a hidden pattern that was totally missing before: we're not looking at one bell curve, but at two different bell curves that partially overlap. This isn't surprising: men and women have different mean heights. We might expect to see the same bell curve structure in the weights for both genders, so let's make a new density plot for the weights column of our data set:

```
ggplot(heights.weights, aes(x = Weight, fill = Gender)) + geom_density()
```

Looking at Figure 2-10, we see the same mixture of bell curves structure. In future chapters, we'll cover this sort of mixture of bell curves in some detail, but it's worth giving a name to the structure we're looking at right now: it's a mixture model in which two standard distributions have been mixed to produce a non-standard distribution.

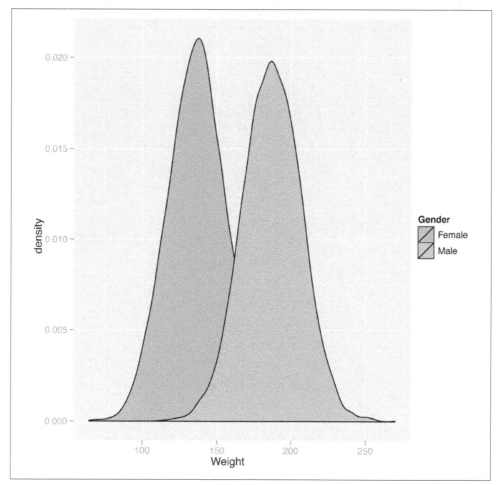

Figure 2-10. Density plot of 10,000 people's weights in pounds with genders

Of course, we need to describe our standard distributions more clearly to give sense to that sentence, so let's start with our first idealized data distribution: the normal distribution, which is also called the Gaussian distribution or the bell curve. We can easily see an example of the normal distribution by simply splitting up the plot into two pieces, called facets. We'll do this with the density plots we've shown you so far so that you can see the two bell curves in isolation from one another. In R, we can build this sort of faceted plot as follows:

```
ggplot(heights.weights, aes(x = Weight, fill = Gender)) + geom_density() +
    facet_grid(Gender ~ .)
```

Once we've run this code, we can look at Figure 2-11 and clearly see one bell curve centered at 64" for women and another bell curve centered at 69" for men. This specific bell curve is the normal distribution, a shape that comes up so often that it's easy to think that it's the "normal" way for data to look. This isn't quite true: lots of things we care about, from people's annual incomes to the daily changes in stock prices, aren't very well described using the normal distribution. But the normal distribution is very important in the mathematical theory of statistics, so it's much better understood than most other distributions.

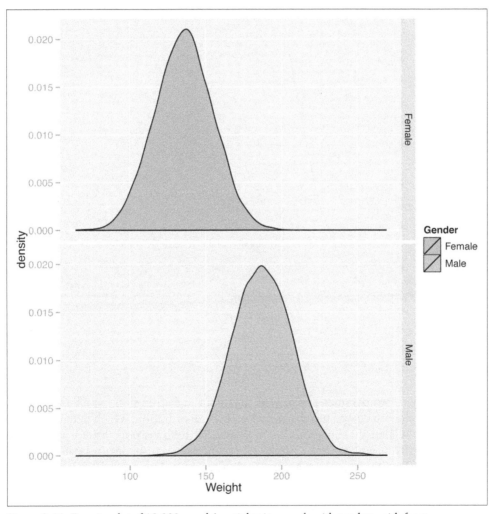

Figure 2-11. Density plot of 10,000 people's weights in pounds with genders, with facets

On a more abstract level, a normal distribution is just a type of bell curve. It might be any of the bell curves shown in Figures 2-12 through Figure 2-14.

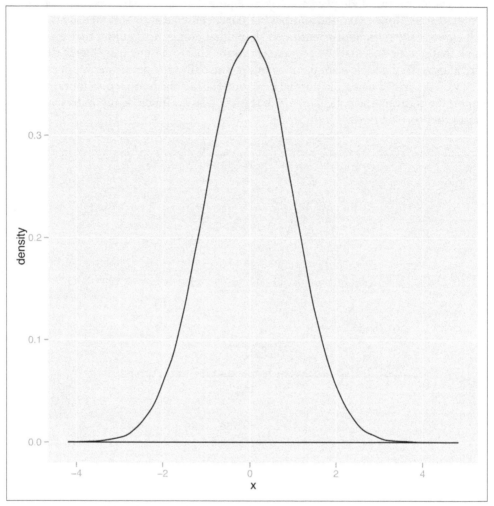

Figure 2-12. Normal distribution with mean 0 and variance 1

In these graphs, two parameters vary: the mean of the distribution, which determines the center of the bell curve, and the variance of the distribution, which determines the width of the bell curve. You should play around with visualizing various versions of the bell curve by playing with the parameters in the following code until you feel comfortable with how the bell curve looks. To do that, play with the values of m and s in the code below:

```
m <- 0
s <- 1
ggplot(data.frame(X = rnorm(100000, m, s)), aes(x = X)) + geom_density()
```

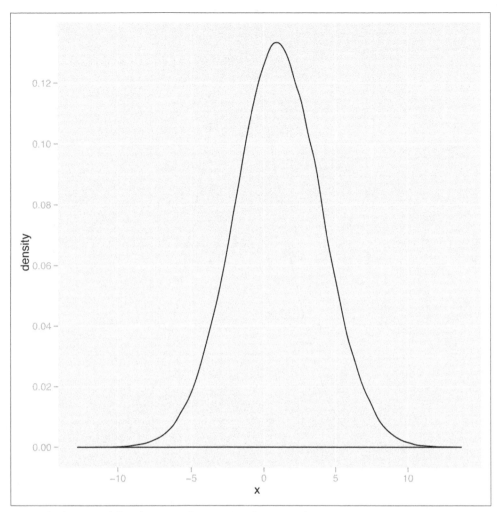

Figure 2-13. Normal distribution with mean 1 and variance 3

All of the curves you can generate with this code have the same basic shape: changing m and s only moves the center around and contracts or expands the width. Unfortunately, seeing this general bell shape isn't sufficient to tell you that your data is normal: there are other bell-shaped distributions, one of which we'll describe in just a moment. For now, let's do a quick jargon lesson, since the normal distribution lets us define several qualitative ideas about the shape of data.

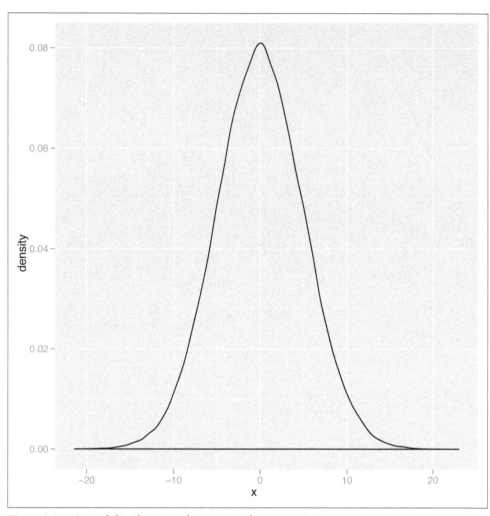

Figure 2-14. Normal distribution with mean 0 and variance 5

Modes

First, let's return to the topic of modes that we put off until now. As we said earlier, the mode of a continuous list of numbers isn't well defined, since no numbers repeat. But the mode has a clear visual interpretation: when you make a density plot, the mode of the data is the peak of the bell. For an example, look at Figure 2-15.

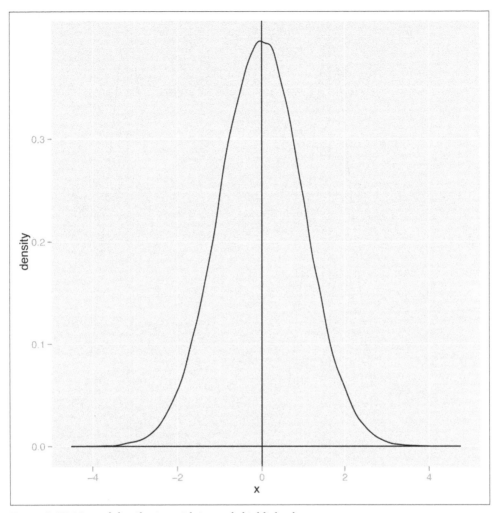

Figure 2-15. Normal distribution with its mode highlighted

Estimating modes visually is much easier to do with a density plot than with a histogram, which is one of the reasons we prefer density plots over histograms. And modes make sense almost immediately when you look at density plots, whereas they often make very little sense if you try to work with the numbers directly.

Now that we've defined a mode, we should point out one of the defining traits of the normal distribution is that it has a single mode, which is also the mean and the median of the data it describes. In contrast, a graph like the one shown in Figure 2-16 has two modes, and the graph in Figure 2-17 has three modes.

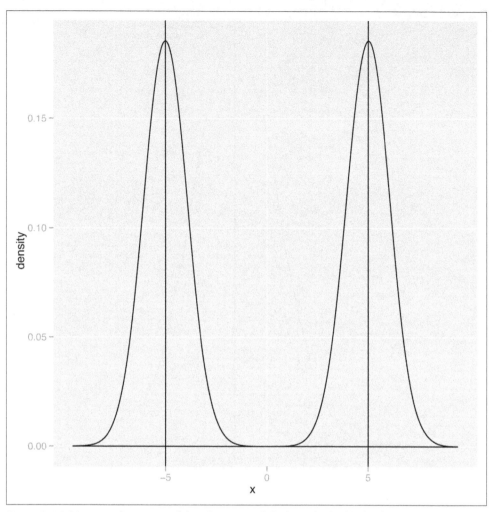

Figure 2-16. Mixture of two normal distributions with both modes highlighted

When we talk about the number of modes that we see in our data, we'll use the following terms: a distribution with one mode is unimodal; a distribution with two modes is bimodal; and a distribution with two or more modes is multimodal.

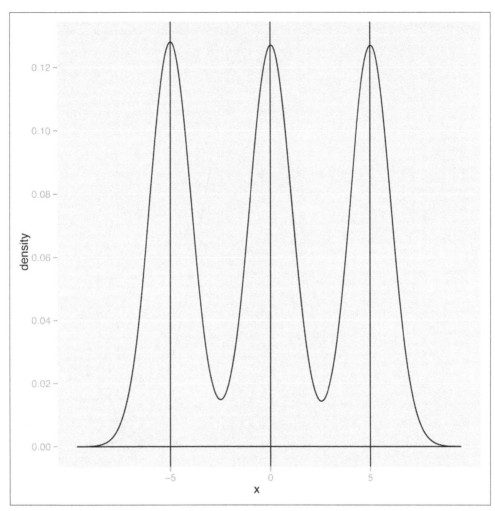

Figure 2-17. Mixture of three normal distributions with three modes highlighted

Skewness

Another important qualitative distinction can be made between data that's symmetric and data that's skewed. Figures 2-18 and 2-19 show images of symmetric and skewed data to make these terms clear.

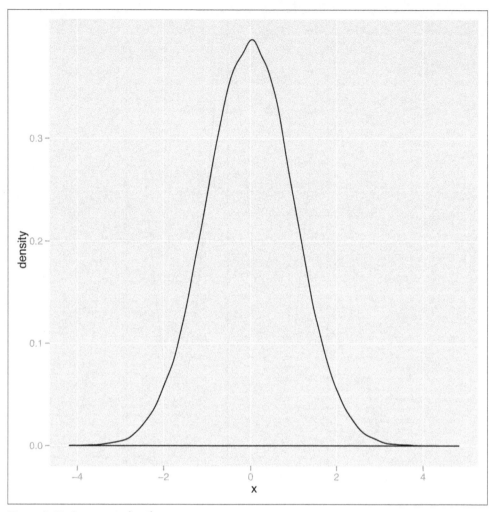

Figure 2-18. Symmetric distribution

A symmetric distribution has the same shape whether you move to the left of the mode or to the right of the mode. The normal distribution has this property, which tells us that we're as likely to see data that's below the mode as we are to see data that's above the mode. In contrast, the second graph, which is called the gamma distribution, is skewed to the right: you're much more likely to see extreme values to the right of the mode than you are to see extreme values to the left of the mode.

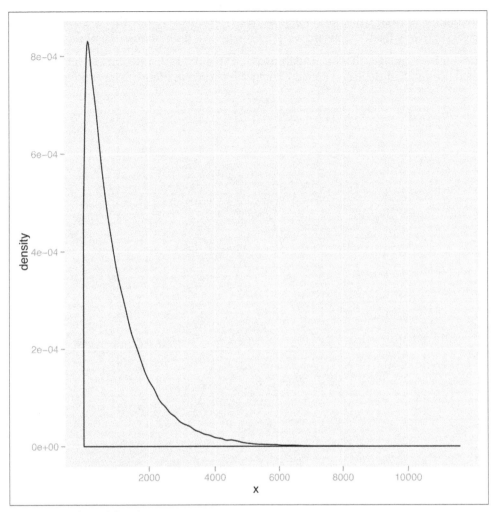

Figure 2-19. Skewed distribution

Thin Tails vs. Heavy Tails

The last qualitative distinction we'll make is between data that's thin-tailed and data that's heavy-tailed. We'll show the standard graph that's meant to illustrate this distinction in a second, but this distinction is probably easier to make in words: a thin-tailed distribution usually produces values that are not far from the mean: let's say that it does so 99% of the time. The normal distribution, for example, produces values that are no more than three standard deviations away from the mean about 99% of the time. In contrast, another bell shaped distribution called the Cauchy distribution produces only 90% of its values inside those three standard deviation bounds. And, as you get further away from the mean value, the two types of distributions become even more different: a normal distribution almost never produces values that are six standard deviations away from the mean, while a Cauchy will do it almost 5% of the time.

The canonical images that are usually used to explain this distinction between the thin-tailed normal and the heavy-tailed Cauchy are shown in Figure 2-20 and Figure 2-21.

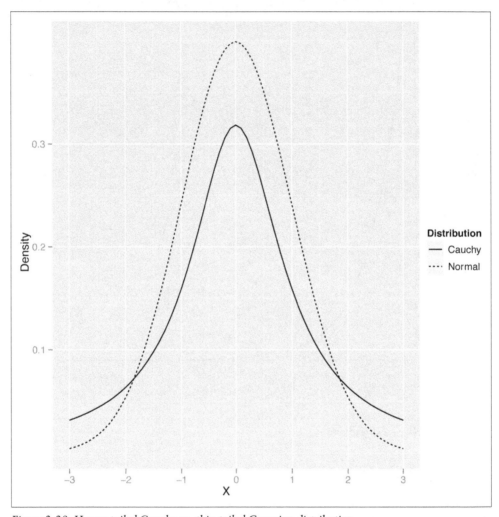

Figure 2-20. Heavy-tailed Cauchy vs. thin-tailed Gaussian distribution

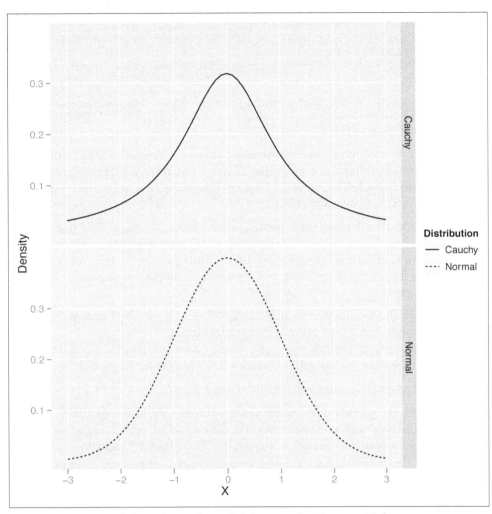

Figure 2-21. Heavy-tailed Cauchy vs. thin-tailed Gaussian distribution, with facets

But we think you'll get more intuition by just generating lots of data from both of those distributions and seeing the results for yourself. R makes this quite easy, so you should try the following:

```
set.seed(1)
normal.values <- rnorm(250, 0, 1)
cauchy.values <- rcauchy(250, 0, 1)

range(normal.values)
range(cauchy.values)
```

Plotting these will also make the point clearer:

```
df <- data.frame(X = c(x, x), Distribution = c(rep('Normal', length(x)), rep('Cauchy',
length(x))), Density = c(y, z))
ggplot(df, aes(x = X, y = Density, linetype = Distribution, group = Distribution)) +
  geom_line()

ggplot(df, aes(x = X, y = Density, linetype = Distribution, group = Distribution)) +
  geom_line() +
  facet_grid(Distribution ~ .)
```

To end this section on the normal distribution and its cousin the Cauchy distribution, let's summarize the qualitative properties of the normal once more: it's unimodal, symmetric, and has a bell shape with thin tails. The Cauchy is unimodal, symmetric, and has a bell shape with heavy tails.

After the normal distribution, there are two more canonical images we want to show you before we bring this section on density plots to a close: a mildly skewed distribution called the gamma and a very skewed distribution called the exponential. We'll use both later on since they occur in real data, but it's worth describing them now to illustrate the skew visually.

Let's start with the gamma distribution. It's quite flexible, so we'd encourage you to play with it on your own for a bit. Here's a starting point:

```
gamma.values <- rgamma(100000, 1, 0.001)
ggplot(data.frame(X = gamma.values), aes(x = X)) + geom_density()
```

The resulting plot of the gamma data is shown in Figure 2-22.

As you can see, the gamma distribution is skewed to the right, which means that the median and the mean can sometimes be quite different. In Figure 2-23, we've plotted some scores we spidered from people playing the iPhone game Canabalt.

This real data set looks remarkably like data that could have been produced by a theoretical gamma distribution. We also bet that you'll see this sort of shape in the density plots for scores in lot of other games as well, so it seems like a particularly useful theoretical tool to have in your belt if you want to analyze game data.

One other thing to keep in mind is that the gamma distribution only produces positive values. When we describe how to use stochastic optimization tools near the end of this book, having an all positive distribution will come in very handy.

The last distribution we'll describe is the exponential distribution, which is a nice example of a powerfully skewed distribution. An example data set drawn from the exponential distribution is shown in Figure 2-24.

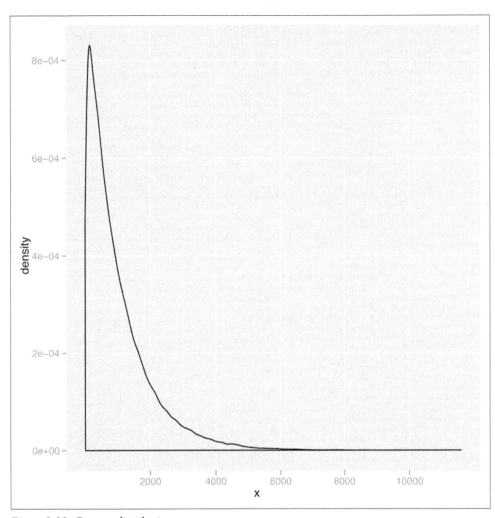

Figure 2-22. Gamma distribution

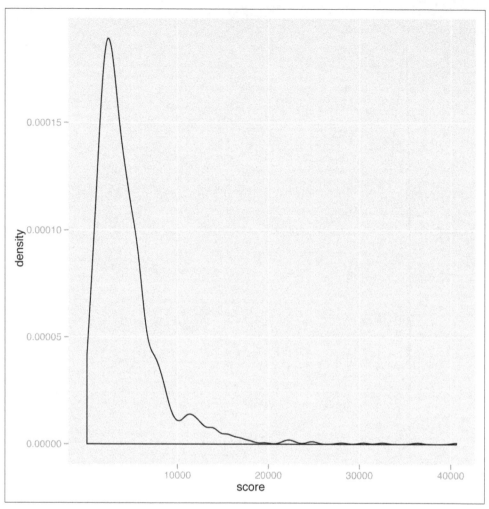

Figure 2-23. Canabalt scores

Because the mode of the exponential distribution occurs at zero, it's almost like you had cut off the positive half of a bell to produce the exponential curve. This distribution comes up quite a lot when the most frequent value in your data set is zero and only positive values can ever occur. For example, corporate call centers often find that the length of time between the calls they receive looks like an exponential distribution.

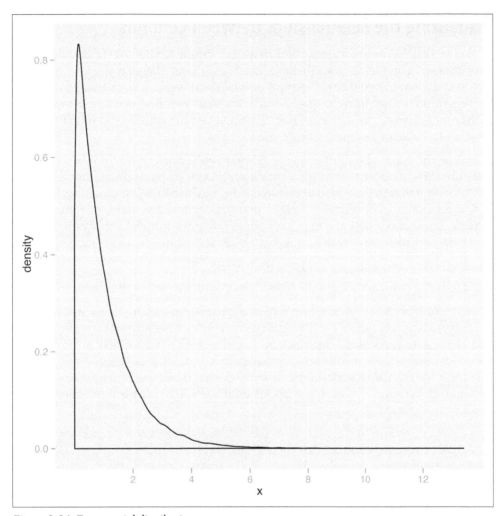

Figure 2-24. Exponential distribution

As you build up a greater familiarity with data and learn more about the theoretical distributions that statisticians have studied, these distributions will become more familiar to you — especially because the same few distributions come up over and over again. For right now, what you really take away form this section are the simple qualitative terms that you can use to describe your data to others: unimodal vs. multimodal, symmetric vs. skewed, and thin-tailed vs. heavy-tailed.

Visualizing the Relationships between Columns

So far we've only covered strategies for thinking carefully about individual columns in your data set. This is clearly worth doing: often just seeing a familiar shape in your data tells you a lot about your data. Seeing a normal distribution tells us that you can use the mean and median interchangeably and it also tells you that you can trust that most of the time you won't see data more than three standard deviations away from the mean. That's a lot to learn just from a single visualization.

But all of the material we just reviewed is what you'd expect to learn in a traditional statistics class: it doesn't have the feel of the machine learning applications that you're presumably itching to start getting involved with. To do real machine learning, we need to find relationships between multiple columns in our data and use those relationships to make sense of our data and to predict things about the future. Some examples we'll touch on over the course of this book include the following prediction problems:

1. Predicting someone's weight from their height.
2. Predicting whether an email is spam or not using the text of the email.

These sorts of problems break down into two sorts: regression problems, in which you need to predict some number (like weight) given a bunch of other numbers (like height); and classification problems, in which you need to assign a label, like spam, given a bunch of numbers, like word counts for spammy words such as "viagra" and "cialis". The tools we can use to perform regression and classification are many, but there are two motivating types of data visualizations we'd like you to carry around in your head as we move forward.

The first is the stereotypical regression picture. In the regression picture, we make a scatterplot of our data and see that there's a hidden shape that relates two columns in data set. Returning to our beloved heights and weights data, let's make a scatterplot of weights against heights.

If you're not familiar with them, you should know that a scatterplot is a two-dimensional image in which one dimension corresponds to a variable X and another corresponds to a variable Y. To make our scatterplots, we'll continue using `ggplot`.

```
ggplot(heights.weights, aes(x = Height, y = Weight)) + geom_point()
```

The scatterplot that `ggplot` generates is shown in Figure 2-25.

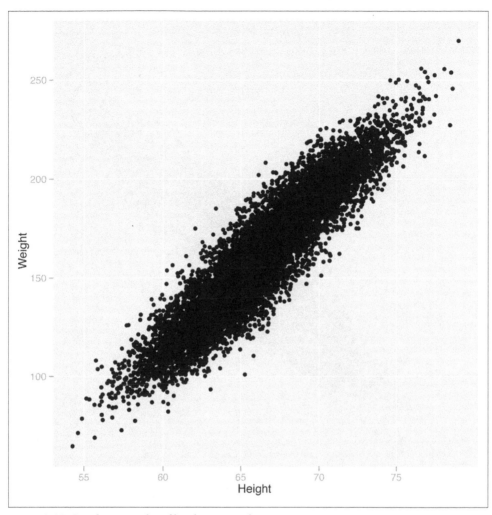

Figure 2-25. Simple scatterplot of heights vs. weights

Looking at this image, it seems pretty clear that there's a pattern relating heights with weights: people who are taller also weigh more. To get started at examining the pattern more carefully, we can use a smoothing tool in `ggplot2` to get a visual depiction of the linear pattern we're seeing:

```
ggplot(heights.weights, aes(x = Height, y = Weight)) + geom_point() + geom_smooth()
```

The new scatterplot with a smooth pattern superimposed is shown in Figure 2-26.

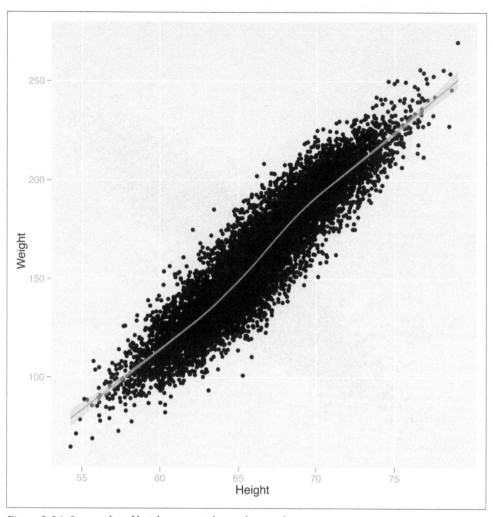

Figure 2-26. Scatterplot of heights vs. weights with smooth pattern

geom_smooth will generate predictions for people's weights given their heights as an input. In this case, the predictions are simply a line. Around the line there is a shaded region, which describes other plausible predictions that could have been made for someone's weight based on the data you've seen. As you get more data, these guesses become more accurate and the shaded region shrinks. Since we already used all of the data, the best way to see the effect happen is to go in the opposite direction: remove some of our data and see how the pattern gets weaker and weaker. The results are shown in Figures 2-27 to Figure 2-29.

```
ggplot(heights.weights[1:20,], aes(x = Height, y = Weight)) + geom_point() +
geom_smooth()
```

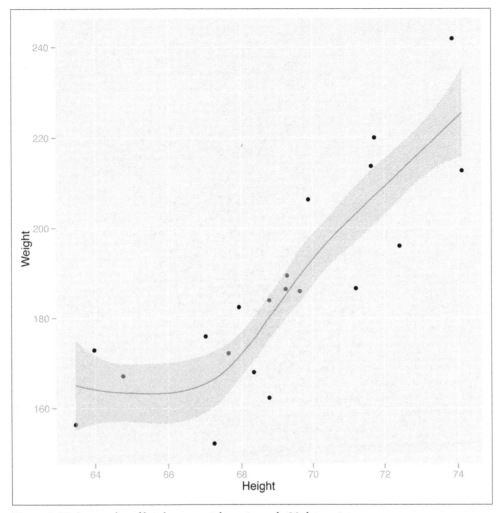

Figure 2-27. Scatterplot of heights vs. weights using only 20 data points

```
ggplot(heights.weights[1:200,], aes(x = Height, y = Weight)) + geom_point() +
geom_smooth()
```

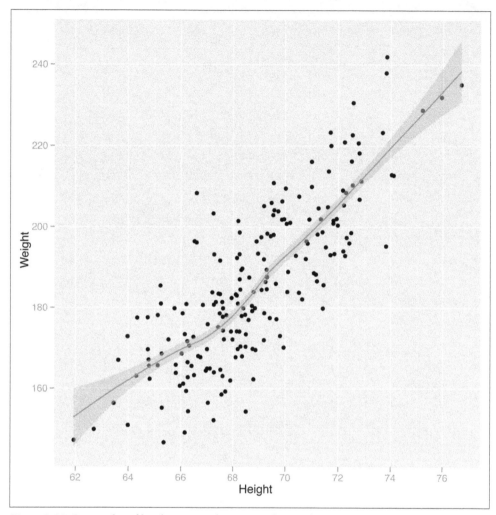

Figure 2-28. Scatterplot of heights vs. weights using only 200 data points

```
ggplot(heights.weights[1:2000,], aes(x = Height, y = Weight)) + geom_point() +
geom_smooth()
```

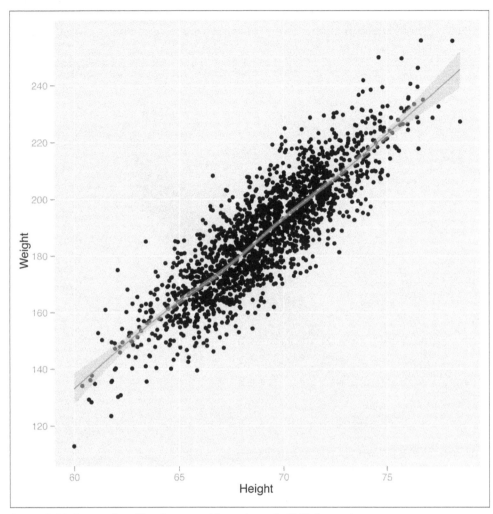

Figure 2-29. Scatterplot of heights vs. weights using only 2000 data points

Recall that predicting the values in one column using another column is called regression when the values you're trying to predict are numbers. In contrast, when you're trying to predict labels, we call that classification. For classification, Figure 2-30 is the image you should keep in mind.

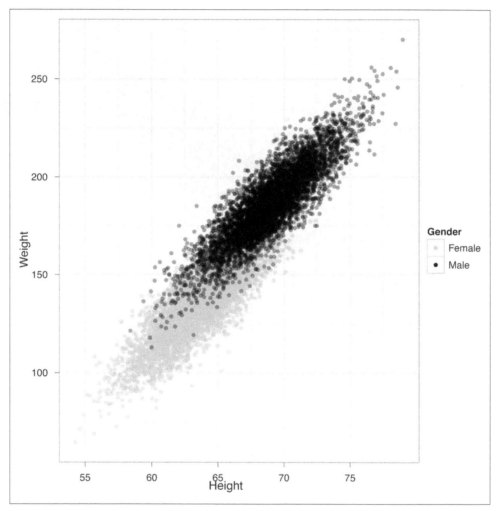

Figure 2-30. Scatterplot of heights vs. weights (classification)

In this image, we've shown the heights and weights of every person in our data set, but we've also visualized their gender as the color of each point. That makes it clear that we see two distinct groups of people in our data. To generate this image in ggplot2, we run the following code:

```
ggplot(heights.weights, aes(x = Height, y = Weight)) + geom_point(aes(color = Gender,
alpha=0.25)) +
    scale_alpha(legend=FALSE)+scale_color_manual(values=c("Male"="black",
"Female"="gray"))+theme_bw()
```

This image is the standard classification picture. In the classification picture, we make a scatterplots of our data, but use a third column to color in the points with different labels. For our height and weight data, we added a third column, which is the sex of each person in our data set. Looking at this picture, it probably seems like we could guess people's gender using only their height and weight. Making guesses about categorical variables like gender from other data is exactly what classification is meant to do and we'll describe algorithms for it in some detail in the next chapter. For now, we'll just show you in Figure 2-31 what the results would look like after running a standard classification algorithm.

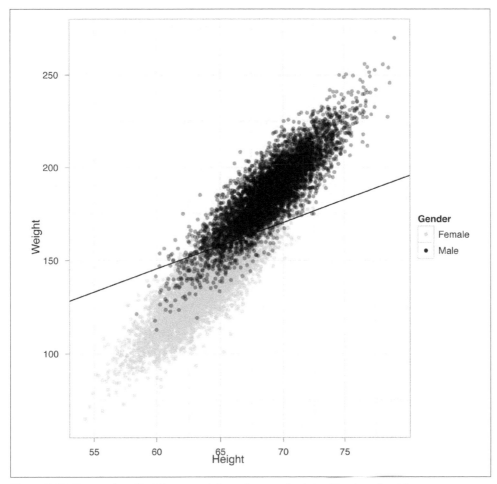

Figure 2-31. Scatterplot of heights vs. weights, after standard classification algorithm

The line we've drawn has a very fancy sounding name: it's called the "separating hyperplane." It's a "separating" hyperplane because it splits the data into two groups: on one side, you guess that someone is female given their height and weight, and on the other side you guess that they're male. This is a pretty good way to make guesses: for this data set, you'd be right about 92% of the time. In our mind, that's not bad performance when you're only using the simplest classification model that's out there, with only heights and weights as inputs to your prediction algorithm. In our real classification tasks, we'll often have tens, hundreds, or even thousands of inputs to use for predicting classes. This data set just happens to be particularly easy to work with, which is why we started with it.

That's the end of this chapter. As a teaser to get you excited for the next chapter, we'll show you the R code that generated the predictions you just saw. As you can see, you need almost no code at all to get pretty impressive results:

```
heights.weights <- transform(heights.weights, Male = ifelse(Gender == 'Male', 1, 0))
logit.model <- glm(Male ~ Weight + Height, data = heights.weights, family =
binomial(link = 'logit'))

ggplot(heights.weights, aes(x = Height, y = Weight)) + geom_point(aes(color = Gender,
alpha=0.25)) +
  scale_alpha(legend=FALSE)+scale_color_manual(values=c("Male"="black",
"Female"="gray"))+theme_bw() +
  stat_abline(intercept = - coef(logit.model)[1] / coef(logit.model)[2],
      slope = - coef(logit.model)[3] / coef(logit.model)[2],
      geom = 'abline',
      color = 'black')
```

In the next chapter, we'll more thoroughly show you how to build your own classifiers using off-the-shelf machine learning tools.

## CHAPTER 3

Classification: Spam Filtering

This or That: Binary Classification

At the very end of the previous chapter, we quickly presented an example of classification. We used heights and weights to predict whether a person was a man or a woman. With our example graph, we were able to draw a line that split the data into two groups: one group where we would predict "male" and another group where we would predict "female." This line was called a separating hyperplane, but we'll use the term "decision boundary" from now on, because we'll be working with data that can't be classified properly using only straight lines. For example, imagine that your data looked like the data set shown in Figure 3-1.

This plot might depict people who are at risk for a certain ailment and those that are not. Above and below the black horizontal lines we might predict that a person is at risk, but inside we would predict good health. These black lines are thus our decision boundary. Suppose that the open circles represent healthy people and the open triangles represent people who suffer from a disease. If that were the case, the two black lines would work quite as a decision boundary for classifying people as healthy or sick.

But before we begin to understand how these decision boundaries are determined in practice, let's review some of the big ideas in classification.

We're going to assume that we have a set of labeled examples of the categories we want to learn how to identify. These examples consist of a label, which we'll also call a class or type, and a series of measured variables that describe each example. We'll call these measurements features or predictors: the height and weight columns we worked with earlier are examples of features that we could use to guess the "male" and "female" labels we were working with before.

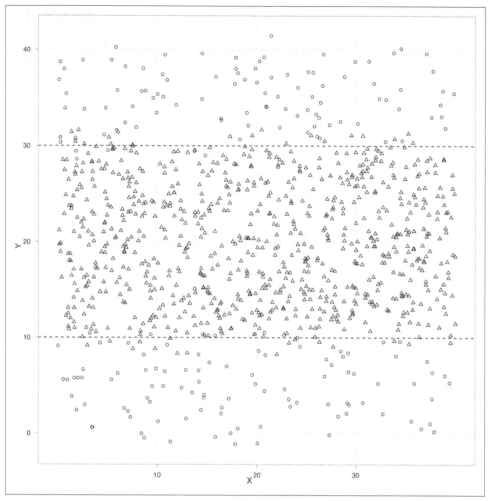

Figure 3-1. Classification with multiple decision boundaries

Examples of classifications can be found anywhere you look for them:

1. Given the results of a mammogram, how do we decide whether a patient has breast cancer or not?
2. Do blood pressure measurements suggest that a patient has hypertension?
3. Does a political candidate's platform suggest that they are a Republican candidate or a Democratic candidate?
4. Does a picture uploaded to a social network contain a face in it or not?
5. Was "The Tempest" written by William Shakespeare or Francis Bacon?

In this chapter, we're going to focus on problems with text classification that are closely related to the tools you could use to answer the last question in our list. In our exercise, however, we're going to build a system for deciding whether an email is spam or ham.

Our raw data are The SpamAssassin Public Corpus, available for free download at: *http://spamassassin.apache.org/publiccorpus/*. Portions of this corpus are included in the *code/data/* folder for this chapter and will be used throughout this chapter. At the unprocessed stage, the features are simply the contents of the raw email as plain text.

This raw text provides us with our first problem. We need to transform our raw text data into a set of features that describe qualitative concepts in a quantitative way. In our case, that will be a 0/1 coding strategy: spam or ham. For example, we may want to determine the following: "does containing HTML tags make an email more likely to be spam?" To answer this, we will need a strategy for turning the text in our email into numbers. Fortunately, the general-purpose text mining packages available in R will do much of this work for us.

For that reason, much of this chapter will focus on building up your intuition for the types of features that people have used in the past when working with text data. *Feature generation* is a major topic in current machine learning research and is still very far from being automated in a general purpose way. At present, it's best to think of the features being used as part of a vocabulary of machine learning that you become more familiar with as you perform more machine learning tasks.

 Just as learning the words of a new language builds up an intuition for what could realistically be a word, learning about the features people have used in the past builds up an intuition for what features could reasonably be helpful in the future.

When working with text, the most important type of feature that's been used historically is word-count. If we think that the text of HTML tags are strong indicators of whether an email is spam, then we might pick terms like "html" and "table" and count how often they occur in one type of document versus the other. To show how this approach would work with the SpamAssassin Public Corpus, we've gone ahead and counted the number of times the terms "html" and "table" occurred: Table 3-1 shows the results.

Table 3-1. Frequency of "spammy" words

Term	Spam	Ham
html	377	9
table	1,182	43

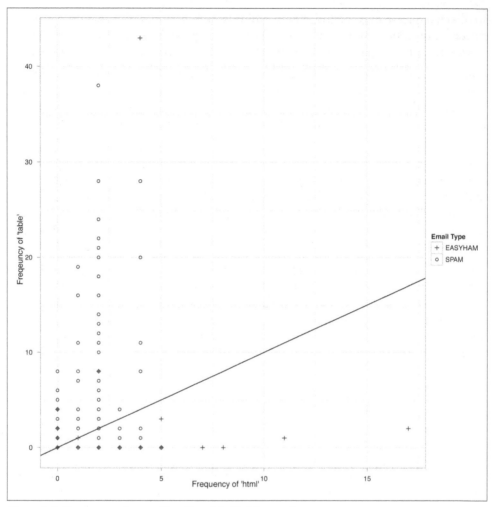

Figure 3-2. Frequency of terms "html" and "table" by email type

For every email in our data set, we've also plotted the class memberships (Figure 3-2). This plot isn't actually very informative, because too many of the data points in our data set overlap. This sort of problem comes up quite often when you work with data that contains only a few unique values for one or more of your variables. As this is a recurring problem, there is a standard graphical solution: we simply add random noise to the values before we plot. This noise will "separate out" the points to reduce the amount of over-plotting. This addition of noise is called *jittering*, and is very easy to produce in `ggplot2` (Figure 3-3).

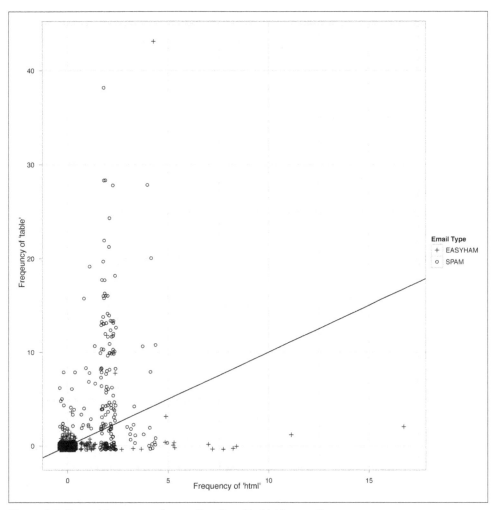

Figure 3-3. Jittered frequency of terms 'html' and 'table' by email type

This last plot suggests that we could do a so-so job of deciding whether an email is spam or not simply by counting the number of times the terms "html" and "table" occur.

The commands used to create the plots in Figure 3-2 and Figure 3-3 begin at line 129 of the *email_classify.R* file in the *code/* folder for this chapter.

In practice, we can do a much better job by using many more than just these two very obvious terms. In fact, for our final analysis we'll use several thousand terms. Even though we'll only use word-count data, we'll still get relatively accurate classification. In the real world, you'd want to use other features beyond word-counts, like falsified headers, IP or email black list, etc.; but here we only wish to introduce the basics of text classification.

Before we can proceed, we should review some basic concepts of conditional probability and discuss how they relate to classifying a message based on its text.

Moving Gently into Conditional Probability

At its core, text classification is a 20th century application of the 18th century concept of *conditional probability*. A conditional probability is the likelihood of observing one thing given some other thing that we already know about. For example, we might want to know the probability that a college student is female, given that we already know the student's major is computer science. This is something we can look up in survey results. According to a National Science Foundation survey in 2005, only 22% of undergraduate computer science majors were female [SR08]. But 51% of undergraduate science majors overall were female, so conditioning on being a computer science major lowers the chances of being a woman from 51% to 22%.

The text classification algorithm we're going to use in this chapter, called the Naive Bayes classifier, looks for differences of this sort by searching through text for words that are either (a) noticeably more likely to occur in spam messages or (b) noticeably more likely to occur in ham messages. When a word is noticeably more likely to occur in one context rather than the other, its occurrence can be diagnostic of whether a new message is spam or ham. The logic is simple: if you see a single word that's more likely to occur in spam than ham, that's evidence that the email as a whole is spam. If you see many words that are more likely to occur in spam than ham and very few words that are more likely to occur in ham than spam, that should be strong evidence that the email as a whole is spam.

Ultimately, our text classifier formalizes this intuition by computing (a) the probability of seeing the exact contents of an email, conditioned on the email being assumed to be spam and (b) the probability of seeing the same email's contents, conditioned on the email being assumed to be ham. If it's much likely that we would see the email in question if it were spam, we'll declare it to be spam.

How much more likely a message needs to be to merit being labeled spam depends upon an additional piece of information: the base rate of seeing spam messages. This base rate information is usually called the prior. You can think of the prior in the following way: if most of the birds you see in the park are ducks and you see a bird quacking one morning, it's a pretty safe bet to assume that it's a duck. But if you have never seen a duck in the park even once, it's much riskier to assume that anything that quacks must be a duck. When working with email, the prior comes into play because the majority of email sent is spam, which means that even weak evidence that an email is spam can be sufficient to justify labeling it as spam.

In the following section we will elaborate on this logic in some detail as we write a spam classifier. To compute the probability of an email being spam, we will assume that the occurrence counts for every word can be estimated in isolation of all of the other words. Formally, this amounts to an assumption often referred to as statistical independence. When we make this assumption without being certain that it's correct, we say that our model is naive. Because we will also make use of base rate information about emails being spam, the model will be also called a Bayes model—in homage to the 18th century mathematician who first described conditional probabilities. Taken together, these two traits make our model a Naive Bayes classifier.

Writing Our First Bayesian Spam Classifier

As we mentioned earlier in this chapter, we will be using the SpamAssassin Public Corpus to both train and test our classifier. These data consist of labelled emails from three categories: "spam," "easy ham," and "hard ham." As you'd expect, hard ham is more difficult to distinguish from spam than the easy stuff. For instance, hard ham messages often include HTML tags. Recall that one way we mentioned to easily identify spam was by these tags. To more accurately classify hard ham, we will have to include more information from many more text features. Extracting these features requires some text mining of the email files and constitutes our initial step in creating a classifier.

All of our raw email files include the headers and the message text. A typical "easy ham" email looks like the example in Example 3-1. You'll note several features of this text that are of interest. First, there is a lot of information about where this email has come from contained in the header. In fact, due to size constraints, we only included a portion of the total header in Example 3-1. And despite the fact that there is a lot of useful information contained in the headers, we will not be using any of this information in our classifier. Rather than focus on features contained in the transmission of the message, we are interested in how the contents of the messages themselves can help predict an email's type. This is not to say that one should always ignore header (or other) information. In fact, all modern sophisticated spam filters utilize information contained in email message headers, such as whether portions of it appear to have been forged, whether the message is from a known spammer, or whether there are bits missing.

Example 3-1. Typical "easy ham" email

```
Received: from usw-sf-list1-b.sourceforge.net ([10.3.1.13]
    helo=usw-sf-list1.sourceforge.net) by usw-sf-list2.sourceforge.net with
    esmtp (Exim 3.31-VA-mm2 #1 (Debian)) id 17hsof-00042r-00; Thu,
    22 Aug 2002 07:20:05 -0700
Received: from vivi.uptime.at ([62.116.87.11] helo=mail.uptime.at) by
    usw-sf-list1.sourceforge.net with esmtp (Exim 3.31-VA-mm2 #1 (Debian)) id
    17hsoM-0000Ge-00 for <spamassassin-devel@lists.sourceforge.net>;
```

Thu, 22 Aug 2002 07:19:47 -0700
Received: from [192.168.0.4] (chello062178142216.4.14.vie.surfer.at
    [62.178.142.216]) (authenticated bits=0) by mail.uptime.at (8.12.5/8.12.5)
    with ESMTP id g7MEI7Vp022036 for
    <spamassassin-devel@lists.sourceforge.net>; Thu, 22 Aug 2002 16:18:07
    +0200
From: David H=?ISO-8859-1?B?9g==?=hn <dh@uptime.at>
To: <spamassassin-devel@example.sourceforge.net>
Message-Id: <B98ABFA4.1F87%dh@uptime.at>
MIME-Version: 1.0
X-Trusted: YES
X-From-Laptop: YES
Content-Type: text/plain; charset="US-ASCII"
Content-Transfer-Encoding: 7bit
X-Mailscanner: Nothing found, baby
Subject: [SAdev] Interesting approach to Spam handling..
Sender: spamassassin-devel-admin@example.sourceforge.net
Errors-To: spamassassin-devel-admin@example.sourceforge.net
X-Beenthere: spamassassin-devel@example.sourceforge.net
X-Mailman-Version: 2.0.9-sf.net
Precedence: bulk
List-Help: <mailto:spamassassin-devel-request@example.sourceforge.net?subject=help>
List-Post: <mailto:spamassassin-devel@example.sourceforge.net>
List-Subscribe: <https://example.sourceforge.net/lists/listinfo/spamassassin-devel>,
    <mailto:spamassassin-devel-request@lists.sourceforge.net?subject=subscribe>
List-Id: SpamAssassin Developers <spamassassin-devel.example.sourceforge.net>
List-Unsubscribe: <https://example.sourceforge.net/lists/listinfo/spamassassin-devel>,
    <mailto:spamassassin-devel-request@lists.sourceforge.net?subject=unsubscribe>
List-Archive: <http://www.geocrawler.com/redir-sf.php3?list=spamassassin-devel>
X-Original-Date: Thu, 22 Aug 2002 16:19:48 +0200
Date: Thu, 22 Aug 2002 16:19:48 +0200

Hello, have you seen and discussed this article and his approach?

Thank you

http://www.paulgraham.com/spam.html
-- "Hell, there are no rules here-- we're trying to accomplish something."
-- Thomas Alva Edison

This sf.net email is sponsored by: OSDN - Tired of that same old
cell phone? Get a new here for FREE!
https://www.inphonic.com/r.asp?r=sourceforge1&refcode1=vs3390

Spamassassin-devel mailing list
Spamassassin-devel@lists.sourceforge.net
https://lists.sourceforge.net/lists/listinfo/spamassassin-devel

Since we are focusing on only the email message body, we need to extract this text from the message files. If you explore some of the message files contained in this exercise, you will notice that the email message *always* begins after the first full line break in the email file. In Example 3-1, we see that the sentence, "Hello, have you seen and discussed this article and his approach?" comes directly after the first line break. To begin building our classifier, we must first create R functions that can access the files and extract the message text by taking advantage of this text convention.

The "null line" separating the header from the body of an email is part of the protocol definition. For reference, see RFC822: *http://tools.ietf .org/html/frc822*.

As is always the case, the first thing to do is to load in the libraries we will use for this exercise. For text classification, we will be using the `tm` package, which stands for *text mining*. Once we have built our classifier and tested it, we will use the `ggplot2` package to visually analyze the results. Another important initial step is to set the path variables for all of the email files. As mentioned, we have three types of messages: easy ham, hard ham, and spam. In the data file directory for this exercise, you will notice that there are two separate sets of file folders for each type of message. We will use the first set of files to train the classifier and the second set to test it.

```
library(tm)
library(ggplot2)

spam.path <- "data/spam/"
spam2.path <- "data/spam_2/"
easyham.path <- "data/easy_ham/"
easyham2.path <- "data/easy_ham_2/"
hardham.path <- "data/hard_ham/"
hardham2.path <- "data/hard_ham_2/"
```

With the requisite packages loaded and the path variables set, we can begin building up our knowledge about the type of terms used in spam and ham by created text corpuses from both sets of files. To do this, we will write a function that opens each file, finds the first line break, and returns the text below that as a character vector with a single text element:

```
get.msg <- function(path) {
    con <- file(path, open="rt", encoding="latin1")
    text <- readLines(con)
    # The message always begins after the first full line break
    msg <- text[seq(which(text=="")[1]+1,length(text),1)]
    close(con)
    return(paste(msg, collapse="\n"))
}
```

The R language performs file I/O in a very similar way to many other programming languages. The function above takes a file path as a string and opens that file in "rt" mode, which stands for *read as text*. Also notice that the coding is "latin1." This is because many of the email messages contain non-ASCII characters, and this encoding will allow us to use these files. The `readLines` function will return each line of text in the file connection as a separate element of a character vector. As such, once we have read in all of the lines, we want to locate the first empty element of the text and then extract all the elements afterward. Once we have the email message as a character vector, we'll close the file connection and then collapse the vector into a single character element using the `paste` function and "\n" (new line) for the `collapse` argument.

To train our classifier, we will need to get the email messages from all of our spam and ham emails. One approach to this is to create a vector containing all of the messages, such that each element of the vector is a single email. The most straightforward way to accomplish this in R is to use an `apply` function with our newly created `get.msg` function:

```
spam.docs <- dir(spam.path)
spam.docs <- spam.docs[which(spam.docs!="cmds")]
all.spam <- sapply(spam.docs, function(p) get.msg(paste(spam.path,p,sep="")))
```

For the spam email, we begin by getting a listing of all of the file names in the `data/spam` directory using the `dir` function. This directory—and all of the directories holding email data—also contain a *cmds* file, which is simply a long list of UNIX base commands to move files in these directories. This is not something we want to include in our training data, so we ignore it by only keeping files that do not have *cmds* as a filename. Now, `spam.docs` is a character vector containing all of the file names for the spam messages we will use to train our classifier.

To create our vector of spam messages, we use the `sapply` function, which will apply `get.msg` to all of the spam file names, and construct a vector of messages from the text returned.

 Note that we have to pass an anonymous function to `sapply` in order to concatenate the file name with the appropriate directory path using the `paste` function. This is a very common construction in R.

Once you have executed this series of commands, you can use the `head(all.spam)` to inspect the results. You will note the name of each vector element corresponds to the file name. This is one of the advantages of using `sapply`.

The next step is to create a text corpus from our vector of emails using the functions provided by the `tm` package. Once we have the text represented as a corpus, we can manipulate the terms in the messages to begin building our feature set for the spam classifier. A huge advantage of the `tm` package is that much of the heavy lifting needed to clean and normalize the text is hidden from view. What we will accomplish in a few lines of R code would take many lines of string processing if we had to perform these operations ourselves in a lower level language.

One way of quantifying the frequency of terms in our spam email is to construct a *term document matrix* (TDM). As the name suggests, a TDM is an N x M matrix in which the terms found among all of the documents in a given corpus define the rows, and all of the documents in the corpus define the columns. The [i, j] cell of this matrix corresponds to the number of times term i was found in document j. As before, we will define a simple function, `get.tdm`, that will take a vector of email messages and return a TDM:

```
get.tdm <- function(doc.vec) {
    doc.corpus <- Corpus(VectorSource(doc.vec))
    control <- list(stopwords=TRUE, removePunctuation=TRUE, removeNumbers=TRUE,
        minDocFreq=2)
    doc.dtm <- TermDocumentMatrix(doc.corpus, control)
    return(doc.dtm)
}

spam.tdm <- get.tdm(all.spam)
```

The tm package allows you to construct a corpus in several ways. In our case, we will be constructing the corpus from a vector of emails, so we will use the VectorSource function. To see the various other source types that can be used, enter ?getSources at the R console. As is often the case when working with tm, once we have loaded our source text we will use the Corpus function in conjunction with VectorSource to create a corpus object. Before we can proceed to creating the TDM, however, we must tell tm how we want it to clean and normalize the text. To do this we use a control, which is a special list of options specifying how to distill the text.

For this exercise we will use four options. First, we set stopwords=TRUE, which tells tm to remove 488 common English stop words from all of the documents. To see the list, type stopwords() at the R console. Next, we set removePunctuation and removeNumbers to TRUE, which are fairly self-explanatory and are used in order to reduce the noise associated with these characters—especially since many of our documents contain HTML tags. Finally, we set minDocFreq=2, which will ensure that only terms that appear more than once in the corpus will end up in the rows of the TDM.

We now have processed the spam emails to the point where we can begin building our classifier. Specifically, we can use the TDM to build a set of training data for spam. Within the context of R, a good approach to doing this is to construct a data frame that contains all of the observed probabilities for each term, given that we know it is spam. Then we need to train our classifier to know the probability an email is spam, given the observation of some term:

```
spam.matrix <- as.matrix(spam.tdm)
spam.counts <- rowSums(spam.matrix)
spam.df <- data.frame(cbind(names(spam.counts),
    as.numeric(spam.counts)), stringsAsFactors=FALSE)
names(spam.df) <- c("term","frequency")
spam.df$frequency <- as.numeric(spam.df$frequency)

spam.occurrence <- sapply(1:nrow(spam.matrix),
    function(i) {length(which(spam.matrix[i,] > 0))/ncol(spam.matrix)})
spam.density <- spam.df$frequency/sum(spam.df$frequency)

spam.df <- transform(spam.df, density=spam.density,
    occurrence=spam.occurrence)
```

To create this data frame, we must first convert the TDM object to a standard R matrix using the `as.matrix` command. Then, using the `rowSums` command, we can create a vector that contains the total frequency counts for each term across all documents. Because we will be combining a character vector with a numeric vector with the `data.frame` function, by default R will convert these vectors to a common representation. Since the frequency counts can be represented as characters, they will be converted, which means we must be mindful to set `stringsAsFactors=FALSE`. Next, we will do some housekeeping to set the column names and convert the frequency counts back to a numeric vector.

With the next two steps, we will generate the critical training data. First, we calculate the percentage of documents in which a given term occurs. We do this by passing every row through an anonymous function call through `sapply`, which counts the number of cells with a positive element and then divides the total by the number of columns in the TDM—i.e., by the number of documents in the spam corpus. Second, we calculate the frequency of each word within the entire corpus. (We will not use the overall frequency information for classification, but it will be useful to see how these numbers compare when we consider how certain words might be affecting our results.)

In the final step, we add the `spam.occurrence` and `spam.density` vectors to the data frame using the `transform` function. We have now generated the training data for spam classification!

Let's check the data and see which terms are the strongest indicators of spam given our training data. To do this, we will sort `spam.df` by the `occurrence` column and inspect its `head`:

```
head(spam.df[with(spam.df, order(-occurrence)),])
       term frequency     density occurrence
2122   html       377 0.005665595      0.338
538    body       324 0.004869105      0.298
4313  table      1182 0.017763217      0.284
1435  email       661 0.009933576      0.262
1736   font       867 0.013029365      0.262
1942   head       254 0.003817138      0.246
```

As we have mentioned repeatedly, HTML tags appear to be the strongest text features associated with spam. Over 30% of the messages in the spam training data contain the term `html`, as well as other common HTML-related terms, such as `body`, `table`, `font`, and `head`. Note, however, that these terms are not the most frequent by raw count. You can see this for yourself by replacing `-occurrence` with `-frequency` in the above statement. This is very important in terms of how we define our classifier. If we used raw count data and the subsequent densities as our training data, we might be over-weighting certain kinds of spam—specifically, spam that contain HTML tables. We know, however, that not all spam are constructed this way. As such, a better approach is to define the conditional probability of a message being spam based on how many messages contain the term.

Now that we have the spam training data, we need to balance it with the ham training data. As part of the exercise, we will build this training data using only the easy ham messages. Of course, it would be possible to incorporate the hard ham messages to the training set; in fact, that would be advisable if we were building a production system. But, within the context of this exercise, it's helpful to see how well a text classifier will work if trained using only a small corpus of easily classified documents.

We will construct the ham training data in exactly the same way we did the spam, and therefore we will not reprint these commands here. The only way this step differs from generating the spam training data is that we only use the first 500 email messages in the data/easy_ham folder.

You may note that there are actually 2,500 ham emails in this directory. So why are we ignoring 4/5 of the data? When we construct our first classifier, we will assume that each message has an equal probability of being ham or spam. As such, it is good practice to ensure that our training data reflect our assumptions. We only have 500 spam messages, so we will limit our ham training set to 500 messages as well.

 To see how we limited the ham training data in this way, see line 102 in the *email_classify.R* file for this chapter.

Once the ham training data have been constructed, we can inspect them just as we did the spam:

```
head(easyham.df[with(easyham.df, order(-occurrence)),])
        term frequency     density occurrence
3553   yahoo       185 0.008712853      0.180
966     dont       141 0.006640607      0.090
2343  people       183 0.008618660      0.086
1871   linux       159 0.007488344      0.084
1876    list       103 0.004850940      0.078
3240    time        91 0.004285782      0.064
```

The first thing you will notice in the ham training data is that the terms are much more sparsely distributed among the emails. The term that occurs in the most documents, "yahoo," does so in only 18% of them. The other terms all occur in less than 10% of the documents. Compare this to the top spam terms, which all occur in over 24% of the spam emails. Already, we can begin to see how this variation will allow us to separate spam from ham. If a message contains just one or two terms strongly associated with spam, it will take a lot of non-spam words for the message to be classified as ham. With both training sets defined, we are now ready to complete our classifier and test it!

Defining the Classifier and Testing It with Hard Ham

We want to define a classifier that will take an email message file and calculate the probability that it is spam or ham. Fortunately, we have already created most of the functions and generated the data needed to perform this calculation. Before we can proceed, however, there is one critical complication that we must consider.

To calculate the probability that an email message is spam or ham, we will need to find the terms that are common between the training data and the message in question. We can then use the probabilities associated with these terms to calculate the conditional probability that a message is of the training data's type. This is fairly straightforward, but what do we do with the terms from the email being classified that are not in our training data?

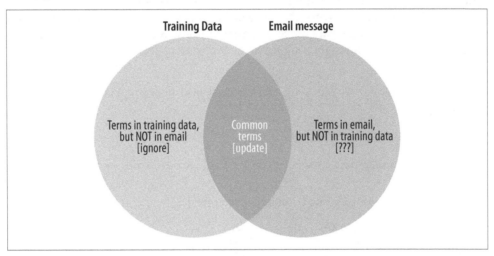

Figure 3-4. How to handle different terms at the training data and message intersection

To calculate the conditional probability of a message, we combine the probabilities of each term in the training data by taking their product. For example, if the frequency of seeing `html` in a spam message is 0.30 and the frequency of seeing `table` in a spam message is 0.10, then we'll say that the probability of seeing both in a spam message is 0.30 * 0.10 = 0.03. But for those terms in the email that are not in our training data, we have no information about its frequency in either spam or ham messages. One possible solution would be to assume that because we have not seen a term yet, its probability of occurring in a certain class is zero. This, however, is very misguided. First, it is foolish to assume that simply because we have not yet seen a term, we will never see it in the entire universe of spam and ham. Moreover, because we calculate conditional probabilities using products, if we assigned a zero probability to terms not in our training data, elementary arithmetic tells us that we would calculate zero as the probability of most messages, since we would be multiplying all the other probabilities by zero every time we encountered an unknown term. This would cause catastrophic results for our classifier, as many, or even all, messages would be incorrectly assigned a zero probability to be either spam or ham.

Researchers have come up with many clever ways of trying to get around this problem, such as drawing a random probability from some distribution or using natural language processing (NLP) techniques to estimate the "spamminess" of a term given its context. For our purposes, we will use a very simple rule: assign a very small probability to terms that are not in the training set. This is, in fact, a common way of dealing with missing terms in simple text classifiers, and for our purposes it will serve just fine. In this exercise, by default we will set this probability to 0.0001%, or one-ten-thousandth of a percent, which is sufficiently small for this data set. Finally, because we are assuming that all emails are equally likely of being ham or spam, we set our default prior belief that an email is of some type to 50%. In order to return to this problem later, however, we construct the `classify.email` function such that the prior belief can be varied.

 Be wary of always using 0.0001% for terms not in the training set. We are using it in this example, but in others it may be too large or too small, and then the system you build will not work at all!

```
classify.email <- function(path, training.df, prior=0.5, c=1e-6) {
    msg <- get.msg(path)
    msg.tdm <- get.tdm(msg)
    msg.freq <- rowSums(as.matrix(msg.tdm))
    # Find intersections of words
    msg.match <- intersect(names(msg.freq), training.df$term)
    if(length(msg.match) < 1) {
        return(prior*c^(length(msg.freq)))
    }
    else {
        match.probs <- training.df$occurrence[match(msg.match, training.df$term)]
        return(prior * prod(match.probs) * c^(length(msg.freq)-length(msg.match)))
    }
}
```

You will notice that the first three steps of the `classify.email` function proceed just as our training phase did. We must extract the message text with `get.msg`, turn it into a term document matrix with `get.tdm`, and finally calculate the frequency of terms with `rowSums`. Next, we need to find how the terms in the email message intersect with the terms in our training data as depicted in Figure 3-4. To do so, we use the `intersect` command, passing the terms found in the email message and those in the training data. What will be returned are those terms in the grey shaded area of Figure 3-4.

The final step of the classification is to determine whether any of the words in the email message are present in the training set. If so, we use them to calculate the probability that this message if of the class in question.

Assume for now that we are attempting to determine if this email message is spam. Now, `msg.match` will contain all of the terms from the email message in our spam training data, `spam.df`. If that intersection is empty, then the length of `msg.match` will be less than zero and we can only update our prior belief by multiplying it with the product of the number of terms in the email with our tiny probability value: c. The result will be that a tiny probability of being spam is assigned to the email.

Conversely, if this intersection is not empty, we need to find those terms from the email in our training data and look up their occurrence probabilities. We use the match function to do the lookup, which will return the term's element position in the term column of our training data. We use these element positions to return the corresponding probabilities from the occurrence column, and return those values to match.probs. We then calculate the *product* of these values and combine it with our prior belief about the email being spam with the term probabilities and the probabilities of any missing terms. The result is our Bayesian estimate for the probability that a message is spam given the matching terms in our training data.

As an initial test, we will use our training data from the spam and easy ham messages to classify hard ham emails. We know that all of these emails are ham, so ideally our classifier will assign higher probability of being ham to all of these messages. We know, however, that hard ham are "hard" to classify because they contain terms that are also associated with spam. That said, let's see how our simple classifier does!

Just as before, we need to get all of the file paths in order; then we can test the classifier for all hard ham messages by wrapping both a spam test and ham test in sapply calls. The vectors hardham.spamtest and hardham.hamtest contain the conditional probability calculations for each hard ham email of being either spam or ham given the appropriate training data. We then use the ifelse command to compare the probabilities in each vector. If the value in hardham.spamtest is greater than that in hardham.hamtest, then the classifier has classified the message as spam; otherwise, it is ham. Finally, we use the summary command to inspect the results:

```
hardham.docs <- dir(hardham.path)
hardham.docs <- hardham.docs[which(hardham.docs != "cmds")]

hardham.spamtest <- sapply(hardham.docs,
    function(p) classify.email(paste(hardham.path, p, sep=""),
    training.df=spam.df))

hardham.hamtest <- sapply(hardham.docs,
    function(p) classify.email(paste(hardham.path, p, sep=""),
    training.df=easyham.df))

hardham.res <- ifelse(hardham.spamtest > hardham.hamtest, TRUE, FALSE)
summary(hardham.res)
```

Table 3-2. Testing our classifier again "hard ham"

Email type	Num. classified as ham	Num. classified as spam
Hard Ham	184	65

Congratulations! You've written your first classifier, and it did *fairly well* at identifying hard ham as non-spam. In this case, we have approximately a 26% false-positive rate. That is, about one-quarter of the hard ham emails are incorrectly identified as spam. You may think this is poor performance, and in production we would not want to offer an email platform with these results, but considering how simple our classifier is, it is doing quite well. Of course, a better test is to see how the classifier performs again not only hard ham, but also easy ham and spam.

Testing the Classifier Against All Email Types

The first step is to build a simple function that will do the probability comparison we did in the previous section, all at once for all emails:

```
spam.classifier <- function(path) {
    pr.spam <- classify.email(path, spam.df)
    pr.ham <- classify.email(path, easyham.df)
    return(c(pr.spam, pr.ham, ifelse(pr.spam > pr.ham, 1, 0)))
}
```

For simplicity's sake, the `spam.classifier` function will determine whether an email is spam based on the `spam.df` and `easyham.df` training data. If the probability that a message is spam is greater than the probability of being ham, it returns one; otherwise, it returns zero.

As a final step in this exercise, we will test the second sets of spam, easy ham, and hard ham using our simple classifier. These steps proceed exactly as they did in previous sections: wrapping the `spam.classifier` function in an `lapply` function, passing email file paths, and building a data frame. As such, we will not reproduce these function calls here, but you are encouraged to reference the *email_classifier.R* file starting at line 158 to see how this is done.

The new data frame contains the likelihoods of being either spam or ham, the classification, and the email type for each message in all three data sets. The new data set is called `class.df`, and we can use the `head` command to inspect its contents:

```
head(class.df)
        Pr.SPAM      Pr.HAM Class    Type
1 2.712076e-307 1.248948e-282 FALSE EASYHAM
2   9.463296e-84  1.492094e-58 FALSE EASYHAM
3   1.276065e-59  3.264752e-36 FALSE EASYHAM
4   0.000000e+00 3.539486e-319 FALSE EASYHAM
5   2.342400e-26  3.294720e-17 FALSE EASYHAM
6 2.968972e-314 1.858238e-260 FALSE EASYHAM
```

From the first six entries, it seems the classifier has done well, but let's calculate the false-positive and false-negative rates for the classifier across all data sets. To do this, we will construct a N x M matrix of our results, where the rows are the actual classification types and the columns are the predicted types. Because we have three types of email being classified into two types, our confusion matrix will have three rows and two columns (Table 3-3).

The columns will be the percent predicted as ham or spam, and if our classifier works perfectly, the columns will read [1,1,0] and [0,0,1] respectively.

Table 3-3. Matrix for classifier results

Email type	% Classified as ham	% Classified as spam
Easy Ham	0.78	0.22
Hard Ham	0.73	0.27
Spam	0.15	0.85

Unfortunately, we did not write a perfect classifier, but the results are still quite good. Similarly to our initial test, we get about a 25% false-positive rate, with our classifier doing slightly better on easy ham than the hard stuff. On the other hand, the false-negative rate is much lower, at only 15%. To get a better sense of how our classifier fared, we can plot the results using a scatter plot, with the predicted probabilities of being ham on the x-axis and spam on the y-axis.

Figure 3-5 shows this scatter plot in log-log scale. A log transformation is done because many of the predicted probabilities are very tiny, while others are not. With this high degree of variance, it is difficult to compare the results directly. Taking logs is a simple way of altering the visual scale to more easily compare values.

We have also added a simple decision boundary to the plots where y = x, or a perfect linear relationship. This is done because our classifier compares the two predicted probabilities and determines the email's type based on whether the probability of being spam is greater than that of ham. All dots above the black diagonal line, therefore, should be spam, and all below ham. As you can see, this is not the case—but there is considerable clustering of message types.

Figure 3-5 also gives some intuition about how the classifier is underperforming in false-positives. There appear to be two general ways it fails. First, there are many hard ham messages that have a positive probability of being spam, but a near-zero probability of being ham. These are the points pressed up against the y-axis. Second, there are both easy and hard ham messages that have a much higher relative probability of being ham. Both of these observations may indicate a weak training data set for ham emails, as there are clearly many more terms that should be associated with ham that currently are not.

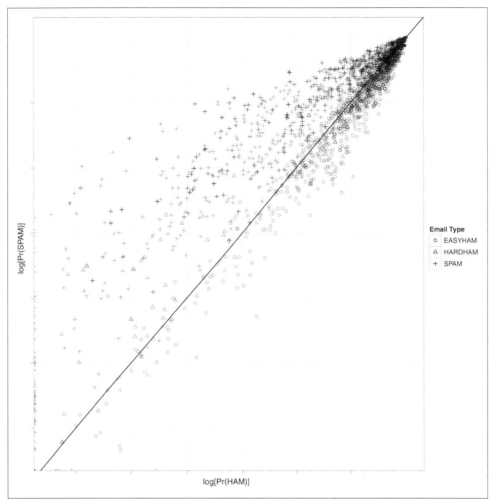

Figure 3-5. Scatter plot of predicted probabilities for email classification in log-log scale

Improving the Results

In this chapter, we introduced the idea of text classification. To do this, we constructed a very simple Bayesian classifier using a minimal number of assumptions and features. This type of classification is—at its core—an application of classic conditional probability theory in a contemporary context. Despite the fact that we trained our classifier with only a fraction of the total available data, this simple method performed reasonably well.

That said, the false-positive and false-negative rates found in the test data are far too high for any production spam filter. As we mentioned throughout the chapter, there are many simple tweaks we could apply to improve the results of the current model. For example, our approach assumes *a priori* that each email has an equal probability of being ham or spam. In practice, however, we know that this relationship is actually much closer to 80%-20% ham-to-spam. One way we might improve results, then, would be to simply alter our prior beliefs to reflect this fact, and recalculate the predicted probabilities:

```
spam.classifier<-function(path) {
    pr.spam<-classify.email(path, spam.df, prior=0.2)
    pr.ham<-classify.email(path, easyham.df, prior=0.8)
    return(c(pr.spam, pr.ham, ifelse(pr.spam > pr.ham, 1, 0)))
}
```

You'll remember that we left the `prior` parameter as something that could vary in the `classify.email` function, so we now only need to make the simple change to `spam.classify` above. We could rerun the classifier now and compare the results, and we encourage you to do so. These new assumptions, however, violate the distributions of ham and spam messages in our training data. To be more accurate, we should go back and retrain the classifier with the complete easy ham data set. Recall that we limited our original ham training data to only the first 500 messages so that our training data would reflect the Bayesian assumptions. In that vein, we must incorporate the full data set in order to reflect our new assumptions.

When we rerun the classifier with the new `easyham.df` and `classify.email` parameterization, we see a notable improvement in performance on false-positives (see Table 3-4).

Table 3-4. Matrix for improved classifier results

Email type	% Classified as ham	% Classified as spam
Easy ham	0.90	0.10
Hard ham	0.82	0.18
Spam	0.18	0.82

With these simple changes, we have reduced our false-positive rate by more than 50%! What is interesting, however, is that by improving performance in this way, our false-negative results suffer. In essence, what we are doing is moving the decision boundaries —recall Figure 3-1. By doing so, we are explicitly trading off false positives for improvement in false negatives. This is an excellent example of why model specification is critical, and how each assumption and feature choice can affect all results.

In the following chapter we will expand our view of classification beyond the simple binary—this or that—example in this exercise. In the next chapter we will explore how to rank emails based on features that are associated with higher priority. What remains important as we increase the spectrum of classification tasks are the features we decide to include in our model. As you'll see next, we may be limited in feature selection by our data, which can have a serious impact on our model design.

## CHAPTER 4

Ranking: Priority Inbox

How Do You Sort Something When You Don't Know the Order?

In Chapter 3, we discussed in detail the concept of *binary classification*—that is, placing items into one of two types or classes. In many cases, we will be satisfied with an approach that can make such a distinction. But what if the items in one class are not created equally, and we want to rank the items within a class? In short, what if we want to say that one email is the most spammy, while another is the second, or we want to distinguish among them in some other meaningful way? Suppose we not only wanted to filter spam from our email, but we also wanted to place "more important" messages at the top of the queue. This is a very common problem in machine learning, and it will be the focus of this chapter.

Generating rules for ranking a list of items is an increasingly common task in machine learning, yet you may not have thought of it in these terms. More likely, you have heard of something like a *recommendation system*, which implicitly produces a ranking of products. Even if you have not heard of a recommendation system, it's almost certain that you have used or interacted with a recommendation system at some point. Some of the most successful e-commerce websites have benefitted from leveraging data on their users to generate recommendations for other products their users might be interested in.

For example, if you have ever shopped at Amazon.com, then you have interacted with a recommendation system. The problem Amazon faces is simple: what items in their inventory are you most likely to buy? The implication of that statement is that the items in Amazon's inventory have an ordering specific to each user. Likewise, Netflix.com has a massive library of DVDs available to its customers to rent. In order for those customers to get the most out of the site, Netflix employs a sophisticated recommendation system to present people with rental suggestions.

For both companies, these recommendations are based on two kinds of data. First, there is the data pertaining to the inventory itself. For Amazon, if the product is a television, this data might contain the type (i.e., plasma, LCD, LED), manufacturer, price, and so on. For Netflix, this data might be the genre of a film, its cast, director, running time, etc. Second, there is the data related to the browsing and purchasing behavior of the customers. This sort of data can help Amazon understand what accessories most people look for when shopping for a new plasma TV and can help Netflix understand which romantic comedies George A. Romero fans most often rent. For both types of data, the features are well identified. That is, we know the labels for categorical data like *product type* or *movie genre*; likewise, user-generated data is well structured in the form of purchase/rental records and explicit ratings.

Because we usually have *explicit examples* of the outputs of interest when doing ranking, this is a type of machine learning problem that is often called *supervised learning*. This is in contrast to *unsupervised learning*, where there are no pre-existing examples of the outputs when we start working with the data. To better understand the difference, think of supervised learning as a process of learning through instruction. For example, if you want to teach someone how to bake a cherry pie, you might hand them a recipe and then let them taste the pie that results. After seeing how the result tastes, they might decide to adjust the ingredients a bit. Having a record of the ingredients they've used (i.e., the inputs) and the taste of the result (i.e., the output) means that they can analyze the contributions of each ingredient and try to find the perfect cherry pie recipe.

Alternatively, if you only knew that dishes with refried beans tend to also come with tortillas, while dishes with baked cherries tend to come with dough, you might be able to group other ingredients into classes that would ultimately resemble the sorts of things you'd use to make Mexican food versus the sorts of things you'd use to make American desserts. Indeed, a common form of unsupervised learning is clustering, where we want to assign items to a fixed number of groups based on commonalities or differences.

If you have already read and worked through the exercise in Chapter 3, then you have already solved a supervised learning problem. For spam classification, we knew the terms associated with spam and ham messages, and we trained our classifier using that recipe. That was a very simple problem, and so we were able to obtain relatively good classification results using a feature set with only a single element: email message terms. For ranking, however, we need to assign a unique weight to each item to stratify them in a finer way.

So in the next section we will begin to address the question proposed in the title of this section: how do you sort something when you don't already know its order? As you may have guessed, to do this in the context of ordering emails by their importance, we will have to reword the question in terms of the features available to us in the email data and how those features relate to an email's priority.

Ordering Email Messages by Priority

What makes an email important? To begin to answer this, let's first step back and think about what email is. First, it is a transaction-based medium. People send and receive messages over time. As such, in order to determine the importance of an email, we need to focus on the transactions themselves. Unlike the spam classification task, where we could use static information from all emails to determine their type, to rank emails by importance we must focus on the dynamics of the in- and out-bound transactions. Specifically, we want to make a determination as to the likelihood a person will interact with a new email once it has been received. Put differently, given the set of features we have chosen to study, how likely is the reader to perform an action on this email in the immediate future?

The critical new dimension that this problem incorporates is *time*. In a transaction-based context, in order to rank things by importance, we need to have some concept of time. A natural way to use time to determine the importance of an email is to measure how long it takes a user to perform some action on an email. The shorter the average time it takes a user to perform some action on an email, given its set of features, the more *important* emails of that type may be.

The implicit assumption in this model is that more important emails will be acted on sooner than less important emails. Intuitively this makes sense. All of us have stared at the queue in our inbox and filtered through emails that needed immediate response versus those that could wait. The filtering that we do naturally is what we will attempt to teach our algorithm to do in the following sections. Before we can begin, however, we must determine which features in email messages are good proxy measures for priority.

Priority Features Email

If you use Google's Gmail service for your email, you will know that the idea of a "priority inbox" was first popularized by Google in 2010. Of course, it was this problem that inspired the case study on ranking for this chapter, so it will be useful to revisit the approach that Google took in implementing their ranking algorithm as we move toward designing our own. Fortunately, several months after the priority inbox feature was released by Google, they published a paper, entitled "The Learning Behind Gmail Priority Inbox," which describes their strategy for designing the supervised learning approach and how to implement it at scale [DA10]. For the purposes of this chapter, we are only interested in the former, but we highly recommend the paper as a supplement to what we discuss here. And at four pages in length, it is well worth the time commitment.

As we mentioned, measuring time is critical, and in Google's case they have the luxury of a long and detailed history of users' interactions with email. Specifically, Google's priority inbox attempts to predict the probability that a user will perform some action on an email within a fixed number of seconds from its delivery. The set of actions a user can perform in Gmail is large: reading, replying, labeling, etc. Also, *delivery* is not explicitly the time at which an email is received by the server, but the time at which it is delivered to the user—i.e., when they check their email.

As with spam classification, this is a relatively simple problem to state: what is the probability that a user will perform some actions, within our set of possible actions, between some minimum and maximum numbers of seconds, given a set of features for that email and the knowledge that the user has recently checked their email?

Within the universe of possible email features, which did Google decide to focus on? As you might expect, they incorporated a very large number of features. As the authors of the paper note, unlike spam classification—which nearly all users will code the same way—everyone has a different way of ordering the priority of email. Given this variability in how users may evaluate the feature set, Google's approach needed to incorporate multiple features. To begin designing the algorithm, Google engineers explored various different types of email features, which they describe as follows:

> There are many hundred features falling into a few categories. *Social features* are based on the degree of interaction between sender and recipient, e.g., the percentage of a sender's mail that is read by the recipient. *Content features* attempt to identify headers and recent terms that are highly correlated with the recipient acting (or not) on the mail, e.g., the presence of a recent term in the subject. Recent user terms are discovered as a pre-processing step prior to learning. *Thread features* note the user's interaction with the thread so far, e.g., if a user began a thread. *Label features* examine the labels that the user applies to mail using filters. We calculate feature values during ranking and we temporarily store those values for later learning. Continuous features are automatically partitioned into binary features using a simple ID3 style algorithm on the histogram of the feature values.

As we mentioned, Google has a long history of its users' interactions with Gmail, which affords them a rich perspective into what actions users perform on emails and when. Unfortunately, such detailed email logs are not available to us in this exercise. Instead, we will again be using the SpamAssassin Public Corpus, available for free download at: *http://spamassassin.apache.org/publiccorpus/*.

Though this data set was distributed as a means of testing spam classification algorithms, it also contains a convenient timeline of a single user's email. Given this single thread, we can repurpose the data set to design and test a priority email ranking system. Also, we will only focus on the ham emails from this data set, so we know that all of the messages we will examine are those that the user would want in their inbox.

Before we can proceed, however, we must consider how our data differs from that of a full-detail email log—such as Google's—and how that affects the features we will be able to use in our algorithm. Let's begin by going through each of the four categories proposed by Google and determining how they might fit into the data we are using.

The most critical difference between a full-detail email log and what we will be working with is that we can only see the messages received. This means that we will be effectively "flying half-blind," as we have no data on when and how a user responded to emails, or if the user was the originator of a thread. This is a **significant limitation**, and therefore the methods and algorithms used in this chapter should be considered as exercises only, and not examples of how enterprise priority inbox systems should be implemented. What we hope to accomplish is to show how, even with this limitation, we can use the data we have to create proxy measures for email importance and still design a relatively good ranking system.

Given that email is a transaction-based medium, it follows that social features will be paramount in assessing the importance of an email. In our case, however, we can only see half of that transaction. In the full-detail case, we would want to measure the volume of interactions between the user and various email senders in order to determine which senders receive more immediate actions from the user. With our data, however, we can only measure incoming volume. We can, then, assume that this one-way volume is a good proxy for the type of social features we are attempting to extract from the data.

Clearly this is not ideal. Recall, however, that for this exercise we will be using only the ham messages from the SpamAssassin Public Corpus. If one receives a large volume of ham email messages from a certain address, then it may be that the user has a strong social connection to the sender. Alternatively, it may be the case that the user is signed up to a mailing list with a high volume and would prefer that these emails not receive a high priority. It is exactly for this reason why we must incorporate other features to balance these types of information when developing our ranking system.

One problem with only looking at the volume of messages from a given address is that the temporal component is protracted. Since our data set is static compared to a fully-detailed email log, we must partition the data into temporal segments and measure volume over these periods to get a better understanding of the temporal dynamics.

As we will discuss in detail later, for this exercise we will simply order all of the messages chronologically, then split the set in half. The first half will be used to train the ranking algorithm and the second half to test. As such, message volume from each email address over the entire time period covered by the training data will be used to train our ranker's social feature.

Given the nature of our data, this may be a good start, but we will need to achieve a deeper understanding if we hope to rank messages more accurately. One way to partition the data to gain a more granular view of these dynamics is to identify conversation threads and then measure the intra-thread activity. (To identify threads, we can borrow techniques used by other email clients and match message subjects with key thread terms, such as "RE:".) The assumption here is that, although we do not know what actions the user is taking on a thread, if it is very active then it is likely to be more important than less-active threads. By compressing the temporal partitions into these small pieces, we can get a much more accurate proxy for the thread features we need to model email priority.

Next, there are many content features we could extract from the emails to add to our feature set. In this case, we will continue to keep things relatively simple by extending the text mining techniques we used in Chapter 3 to this context. Specifically, if there are common terms in the subjects and bodies of emails received by a user, then future emails that contain these terms in the subject and body may be more important than those that do not. This is actually a common technique, and it is mentioned briefly in the description of Google's priority inbox. By adding content features based on terms for both the email subject and body, we will encounter an interesting problem of *weighting*. Typically, there are considerably fewer terms in an email's subject than the body; therefore, we should not weight the relative importance of common terms in these two features equally.

Finally, there are also many features used in enterprise distributed priority inbox implementations—like Gmail's—that are simply unavailable to us in this exercise. We have already mentioned that we are blind to much of the social feature set, and therefore must use proxies to measure these interactions. Furthermore, there are many user actions that we do not even have the ability to approximate. For example, user actions such as labeling or moving email messages are completely hidden from our view. In the Google priority inbox implementation, these actions form a large portion of the action set, but are completely missing here. Again, while this is a weakness to the approach described here when compared to those used when full-detail email logs are available, since they are not available in this case, the fact that they are missing will not affect our results.

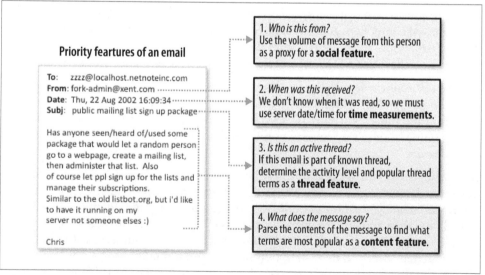

Figure 4-1. Strategy for extracting priority features from email data

We now have a basic blueprint for the feature set we will use to create our email ranking system. We begin by ordering the messages chronologically, because in this case much of what we are interested in predicting is contained in the temporal dimension. The first half of these messages are used to train our ranker. Next, we have four features we will use during training. The first is a proxy for the social feature, which measures the volume of messages from a given user in the training data. Next, we attempt to compress the temporal measurements by looking for threads, and ranking active threads higher than inactive ones. Finally, we add two content features based on frequent terms in email subjects and message bodies. Figure 4-1 is an illustration of how these features are extracted from an email.

In the next section, we will implement the priority inbox approach described above. Using the features listed here, we will specify a weighting scheme that attempts to quickly push more important messages to the top of the stack. As before, however, our first steps will be to take the raw email data and extract the relevant pieces to fit into our feature set.

Writing a Priority Inbox

By now you will have noticed a trend: before we can get to the sexy parts of machine learning, we need to get our hands dirty hacking at the data to split, pull, and parse it until it's in a shape fit for our analysis. So far, we have only had to suffer slightly during this process. To build the spam classifier, we only had to extract the email message body, and then we let the tm package do all of the heavy lifting. For this exercise, however, we are adding several other features to our data set and complicating the process by adding a temporal dimension as well. As such, we will have to operate on the data considerably more. But we are hackers, and getting dirty with data is what we like!

For this exercise, we will be focusing on only the ham email messages from the SpamAssassin Public Corpus. Unlike the spam classification exercise, here we are not concerned with the type of email but rather with how each should be ranked in terms of priority. Therefore, we will use the largest easy ham data set, and not worry about including other types of emails. Since we may safely assume a user would not distinguish among emails in this way when determining which emails have a higher priority, there is no reason to carry this information into our ranking system.[*] Instead, we want to be able to learn as much about our features sets from a single user's emails, which is why we will use the first easy ham data set emails:

```
library(tm)
library(ggplot2)

data.path <- "../../03-Classification/code/data/"
easyham.path <- paste(data.path, "easy_ham/", sep="")
```

---

[*] Put more simply, this is the assumption that users are not acting on emails that were harder to identify as ham than those that were easy.

Similarly to Chapter 3, the only R packages we will be using in this exercise are tm, for extracting common terms from the emails subjects and bodies, and ggplot2, for visualizing the results. Also, since the SpamAssassin Public Corpus is a relatively large text data set, we will not duplicate it in the *data/* folder for this chapter. Instead, we will set the relative path for the data back to its location in the Chapter 3 files.

Next, we will create a series of functions that will work together to parse each email into the feature set illustrated in Figure 4-1. From this diagram we know that we need to extract four elements from each email message: the sender's address, date received, subject, and message body.

Functions for Extracting the Feature Set

Recall that in Chapter 2, we introduced the idea of data as rectangles. For this exercise, therefore, the task of constructing the training data is one of "rectangularization." We need to shape the email data set to fit into a usable feature set. The features we extract from the emails will be the columns of our training data, and each row will be the unique values from a single email filling in the rectangle. Conceptualizing data this way is very useful, as we need to take the semi-structured text data in the email messages and turn them into a highly structured training data set that we can use to rank future emails:

```
parse.email <- function(path) {
    full.msg <- msg.full(path)
    date <- get.date(full.msg)
    from <- get.from(full.msg)
    subj <- get.subject(full.msg)
    msg <- get.msg(full.msg)
    return(c(date, from, subj, msg, path))
}
```

To explore this process, we will work backwards and begin by examining the parse.email function. This will call a series of helper functions that extract the appropriate data from each message, and then order these elements into a single vector. The vector created by the command c(date, from, subj, msg, path) constitutes the single row of data that will populate our training data. The process of turning each email message into these vectors, however, requires some classic text hacking.

 We include the path string as the final column because it will make ordering the data easier during the testing phase.

```
msg.full <- function(path) {
    con <- file(path, open="rt", encoding="latin1")
    msg <- readLines(con)
    close(con)
    return(msg)
}
```

If you worked through the entire case study in Chapter 3, the `msg.full` function above will look very familiar. Here, we are simply opening a connection file path and reading the file's contents into a character vector. The `readLines` function will produce a vector whose elements are each line in the file. Unlike what we did in Chapter 3, here we do not preprocess the data at this step because we need to extract various elements from the messages. Instead, we will return the entire email as a character vector and write separate functions to work on this vector to extract the necessary data.

With the message vector in hand, we must begin to fight our way through the data in order to extract as much useable information from the email messages—and organize them in a uniform way—to build our training data. We will begin with the relatively easy task of extracting the sender's address. To do this—and all of the data extraction in this section—we need to identify the text patterns in the email messages that identify the data we are looking for. To do so, let's take a look at a few email messages.

Example 4-1. Examples of email "From" text pattern variation

    Email #1

    ....

    X-Sender: fortean3@pop3.easynet.co.uk (Unverified)
    Message-Id: <p05100300ba138e802c7d@[194.154.104.171]>
    To: Yahoogroups Forteana <zzzzteana@yahoogroups.com>
    From: Joe McNally <joe@flaneur.org.uk>
    X-Yahoo-Profile: wolf_solent23
    MIME-Version: 1.0
    Mailing-List: list zzzzteana@yahoogroups.com; contact
       forteana-owner@yahoogroups.com

    ....

    Email #2

    ....

    Return-Path: paul-bayes@svensson.org
    Delivery-Date: Fri Sep 6 17:27:57 2002
    From: paul-bayes@svensson.org (Paul Svensson)
    Date: Fri, 6 Sep 2002 12:27:57 -0400 (EDT)
    Subject: [Spambayes] Corpus Collection (Was: Re: Deployment)
    In-Reply-To: <200209061431.g86EVM114413@pcp02138704pcs.reston01.va.comcast.net>
    Message-ID: <Pine.LNX.4.44.0209061150430.6840-100000@familjen.svensson.org>

    ....

After exploring a few email messages, we can observe key patterns in the text that identify the sender's email address. Example 4-1 shows two excerpts from emails that highlight these patterns. First, we need to identify the line in each message that contains the email address. From the examples above, we can see that this line **always** has the term "From:", which again, is specified by the email protocol mentioned in Chapter 3. So, we will use this information to search the character vector for each email to identify the correct element. As we can see from Example 4-1, however, there is variation in how the email address is written among emails. This line always contains the name of the sender and the sender's email address, but sometimes encapsulated in angled brackets (Email #1) while in others it is not enclosed in brackets (Email #2). For that reason, we will write a `get.from` function that uses regular expressions to extract the data for this feature:

```
get.from <- function(msg.vec) {
    from <- msg.vec[grepl("From: ", msg.vec)]
    from <- strsplit(from, '[":<> ]')[[1]]
    from <- from[which(from !="" & from !=" ")]
    return(from[grepl("@", from)][1])
}
```

As we have already seen, R has many powerful functions for working with regular expressions. The grepl function works just like a regular grep function for matching regular expression patterns, but the "l" stands for *logical*. So, rather than returning vector indices, it will return a vector of the same length as msg.vec with boolean values indicating whether the pattern was matched in the character vector. After the first line in this function, the from variable is a character vector with a single element: the "From:" lines highlighted in Example 4-1.

Now that we have the correct line, we need to extract the address itself. To do this, we will use the strsplit function, which will split a character element into a list by a given regular expression pattern. In order to properly extract the addresses, we need to account for the variation in the text patterns observed in Example 4-1. To do so, we create a set of characters for our pattern by using the square brackets. Here, the characters we want to split the text by are colons, angle brackets, and an empty character. This pattern will always put the address as the first element in the list, so we can pull that from the list with [[1]]. Because of the variation in the pattern, however, it will also add empty elements to this vector. In order to return only the email address itself, we will ignore those empty elements, then look for the remaining element containing the "@" symbol, and return that. We now have parsed 1/4 of the data needed to generate our training data.

Extracting the next two features, the message subject and body, is relatively simple. In Chapter 3, we needed to extract the message body in order to quantify the terms in spam and ham email messages. The get.msg function, therefore, simply replicates the pattern we used to perform the same task here. Recall, the message body always appears after the first empty line break in the email. So, we simply look for the first empty element in msg.vec and return all of the elements after that. To simplify the text mining process, we collapse these vectors into a single character vector with the paste function and return that:

```
get.msg <- function(msg.vec) {
    msg <- msg.vec[seq(which(msg.vec == "")[1] + 1, length(msg.vec), 1)]
    return(paste(msg, collapse="\n"))
}
```

Extracting the email's subject is akin to extracting the sender's address, but is actually a bit simpler. With the get.subject function we will again use the grepl function to look for the "Subject:" pattern in each email to find the line in the message that contains the subject. There is, however, a catch: as it turns out, not every message in the data set actually has a subject. As such, the pattern matching we are using will blow up on these edge cases. In order to guard against this, we will simply test to see if our call to grep1 has actually returned anything. To test this, we check that the length of subj is greater than zero. If it is, we split the line based on our pattern and return the second element. If not, we return an empty character. By default in R, when matching functions like grep1 do not make a match, special values such as integer(0) or character(0) will be returned. These values have a zero length, so this type of check is always a good idea when running a function over a lot of messy data:

```
get.subject <- function(msg.vec) {
    subj <- msg.vec[grepl("Subject: ", msg.vec)]
    if(length(subj) > 0) {
        return(strsplit(subj, "Subject: ")[[1]][2])
    }
    else {
        return("")
    }
}
```

 In the *code/data/hard_ham/* folder in the files for Chapter 3, see file 00175.* for a problematic email message. As is often the case when attempting to work a data set into your problem, you will run into edge cases like this. Getting through them will take some trial and error, as it did for us in this case. The important thing is to stay calm and dig deeper into the data to find the problem. You're not doing it right if you do not stumble on your way to parsing a data set into a workable form!

We now have three-quarters of our features extracted, but it is the final element—the date and time the message was received—that will cause us to suffer the most. This field will be difficult to work with for two reasons. First, dealing with dates is almost always a painful prospect, as different programming languages often have slightly different ways of thinking about time; and, in this case, R is no different. Eventually, we will want to convert the date strings into POSIX date objects in order to sort the data chronologically. But to do this, we need a common character representation of the dates, which leads directly to the second reason for our suffering: there is considerable variation within the SpamAssassin Public Corpus in how the dates and times messages received are represented. Example 4-2 illustrates a few examples of this variation.

Example 4-2. Examples of email date and time received text pattern variation

Email #1

....

Date: Thu, 22 Aug 2002 18:26:25 +0700

   Date: **Wed, 21 Aug 2002 10:54:46 -0500**
   From: Chris Garrigues lt;cwg-dated-1030377287.06fa6d@DeepEddy.Comgt;
   Message-ID: lt;1029945287.4797.TMDA@deepeddy.vircio.comgt;
....

Email #2

....
List-Unsubscribe: lt;https://example.sourceforge.net/lists/listinfo/sitescooper-talkgt;,
   lt;mailto:sitescooper-talk-request@lists.sourceforge.net?subject=unsubscribegt;
List-Archive: lt;http://www.geocrawler.com/redir-sf.php3?list=sitescooper-talkgt;

X-Original-Date: 30 Aug 2002 08:50:38 -0500
Date: 30 Aug 2002 08:50:38 -0500

....

Email #3

....

Date: Wed, 04 Dec 2002 11:36:32 GMT
Subject: [zzzzteana] Re: Bomb Ikea
Reply-To: zzzzteana@yahoogroups.com
Content-Type: text/plain; charset=US-ASCII

....

Email #4

....

Path: not-for-mail
From: Michael Hudson lt;mwh@python.netgt;
Date: 04 Dec 2002 11:49:23 +0000
Message-Id: lt;2madyyyyqa0s.fsf@starship.python.netgt;

....

As you can see, there are many things that we need to be cognizant of when extracting the date and time information from each email. The first thing to notice from the examples in Example 4-2 is that the data we want to extract is always identified by "Date:". However, there are many traps in using this pattern that we must be mindful of. As Email #1 from Example 4-2 illustrates, sometimes there will be multiple lines that match this pattern. Likewise, Email #2 shows that some lines may be partial matches, and in either case the data on these lines can be conflicting—as it is in Email #1. Next, we can observe even in these three examples that dates and times are not stored in a uniform way across all emails. In all emails, there are extraneous GMT offsets and other types of labeling information. Finally, the format for the date and time in Email #4 is totally different from the previous two.

All of this information will be critical in getting the data into a uniform and workable form. For now, however, we will only need to focus on extracting the date and time information without the extraneous offset information by defining a `get.date` function. Once we have all of the date/time strings, we will need to deal with converting the conflicting date/time formats to a uniform POSIX object, but this will not be handled by the `get.date` function:

```
get.date <- function(msg.vec) {
    date.grep <- grepl("^Date: ", msg.vec)
    date.grepl <- which(date.grep == TRUE)
    date <- msg.vec[date.grep[1]]
    date <- strsplit(date, "\\+|\\-|: ")[[1]][2]
    date <- gsub("^\\s+|\\s+$", "", date)
    return(strtrim(date, 25))
}
```

As we mentioned, many emails have multiple full or partial matches to the "Date:" pattern. Notice, however, from Emails #1 and #2 in Example 3-1 that only one line from the email has "Date:" at the start of the string. In email #1, there are several empty characters preceding this pattern, and in #2 the pattern is partially matched to "X-Original-Date:". We can force the regular expression to match only strings that have

"Date:" at the start of the string by using the caret operator ("^Date:"). Now, grepl will only return TRUE when that pattern starts an element of the message vector.

Next, we want to return the first element in msg.vec that matches this pattern. We may be able to get away with simply returning the element in msg.vec that matches our pattern in grepl, but what if an email message contains a line that begins "Date:"? If this edge case were to occur, we know the first element that matched our pattern will come from the message's header because header information always comes before the message body. To prevent this problem, we always return the first matching element.

Now we need to process this line of text in order to return a string that can eventually be converted into a POSIX object in R. We've already noted that there is extraneous information and that the dates and times are not stored in a uniform format. To isolate the date and time information, we will split the string by characters that denote extraneous information. In this case, that will be a colon, a plus, or a minus character. In most cases, this will leave us with only the date and time information, plus some trailing empty characters. The use of the gsub function in the next line will substitute any leading or training whitespace in the character string. Finally, to deal with the kind of extraneous data we observe in Email #3 in Example 4-2, we will simply trim off any characters after a 25 character limit. A standard data/time string is 25 characters long, so we know that anything over this is extraneous.

```
easyham.docs <- dir(easyham.path)
easyham.docs <- easyham.docs[which(easyham.docs != "cmds")]
easyham.parse <- lapply(easyham.docs, function(p)
    {parse.email(paste(easyham.path, p, sep=""))})


ehparse.matrix <- do.call(rbind, easyham.parse)
allparse.df <- data.frame(ehparse.matrix, stringsAsFactors=FALSE)
names(allparse.df) <- c("Date", "From.EMail", "Subject", "Message", "Path")
```

Congratulations, you have successfully suffered though transforming this amorphous set of emails into a structured rectangle suitable for training our ranking algorithm! Now all we have to do is throw the switch. Similar to what we did in Chapter 3, we will create a vector with all of the "easy ham" files, remove the extra "cmds" file from the vector, and then use the lapply function to apply the parse.email function to each email file. Because we are pointing to files in the data directory for the previous chapter, we also have to be sure to concatenate the relative path to these files using the paste function and our easyham.path inside the lapply call.

Next, we need to convert the list of vectors returned by lapply into a matrix—i.e., our data rectangle. As before, we will use the do.call function with rbind to create the ehparse.matrix object. We will then convert this to a data frame of character vectors, and then set the column names to c("Date", "From.EMail", "Subject", "Message", "Path"). To check the results, use head(allparse.df) to inspect the first few rows of the data frame. We will not reproduce this here to conserve space, but we recommend you do.

Before we can proceed to creating a weighting scheme from this data, however, there is still some remaining housekeeping.

As we mentioned, our first trial with extracting the dates was simply isolating the text. Now, we need to take that text and convert it into POSIX objects that can be compared logically. This is necessary because we need to sort the emails chronologically. Recall that running through this entire exercise is the notion of *time*, and how temporal differences among observed features can be used to infer importance. The character representation of dates and times will not suffice.

As we saw in Example 4-2, there are two variations on the date format. From these examples, Email #3 has a date/time string of the format "Wed, 04 Dec 2002 11:36:32," while Email #4 is of the format "04 Dec 2002 11:49:23". To convert these two strings into POSIX formats, we will need to use the strptime function, but pass it two different date/time formats to make the conversion. Each element of these strings matches a specific POSIX format element, so we will need to specify conversion strings that match these variants:

```
date.converter <- function(dates, pattern1, pattern2) {
    pattern1.convert <- strptime(dates, pattern1)
    pattern2.convert <- strptime(dates, pattern2)
    pattern1.convert[is.na(pattern1.convert)] <-
pattern2.convert[is.na(pattern1.convert)]
    return(pattern1.convert)
}

pattern1 <- "%a, %d %b %Y %H:%M:%S"
pattern2 <- "%d %b %Y %H:%M:%S"

allparse.df$Date <- date.converter(allparse.df$Date, pattern1, pattern2)
```

 R uses the standard POSIX date/time format strings to make these conversions. There are many options for these strings, and we recommend reading through the documentation in the strptime function using the ?strptime command to see all of the options. Here we will only be using a select few, but understanding them in greater depth will be very useful whenever working with dates and times in R.

We need to convert the strings in the Date column of allparse.df to the two different POSIX formats separately, then recombine them back into the data frame to complete the conversion. To accomplish this, we will define the date.converter function to take two different POSIX patterns and a character vector of date strings. When the pattern passed to strptime does not match the string passed to it, the default behavior is to return NA. We can use this to recombine the converted character vectors by replacing the elements with NA from the first conversion with those from the second. Because we know there are only two patterns present in the data, the result will be a single vector with all date strings converted to POSIX objects.

The final bit of cleanup is to convert the character vectors in the *Subject* and *From* email columns to all lowercase. Again, this is done to ensure that all data entries are as uniform as possible before we move into the training phase. Next, we sort the data chronologically using a combination of the `with` and `order` commands in R. (R has a particularly unintuitive way of doing sorting, but this shorthand is something you will find yourself doing very often, so it is best to get familiar with it.) The combination will return a vector of the element indices in ascending chronological order. Then, to order the data frame by these indices, we need to reference the elements of `allparse.df` in that order, and add the final comma before closing the square bracket so all columns are sorted this way:

```
allparse.df$Subject <- tolower(allparse.df$Subject)
allparse.df$From.EMail <- tolower(allparse.df$From.EMail)

priority.df <- allparse.df[with(allparse.df, order(Date)),]

priority.train <- priority.df[1:(round(nrow(priority.df) / 2)),]
```

Finally, we store the first half of the chronologically-sorted data frame as `priority.train ing`. The data in this data frame will be used to train our ranker. Later, we will use the second half of `priority.df` to test the ranker. With the data fully formed, we are ready to begin designing our ranking scheme. Given our feature set, one way to proceed is to define weights for each observed feature in the training data.

Creating a Weighting Scheme for Ranking

Before we can proceed to implementing a weighting scheme, we need to take a brief digression to discuss scales. Consider for a moment your own email activity. Do you interact with roughly the same people on a regular basis? Do you know about how many emails you receive in a day? How many emails do you receive from total strangers in a week? If you are like us, and we suspect most other people, your email activity crudely adheres to the 80/20 cliche. That is, about 80% of your email activity is conducted with about 20% of the total number of people in your address book. So, why is this important?

We need to be able to devise a scheme for weighting the observation of certain features in our data, but because of the potential differences in scale among these observations, we cannot compare them directly. More precisely, we cannot compare their absolute values directly. Let's take the training data that we have just finished parsing. We know that one of the features that we are adding to our ranker is an approximation of social interaction based on the volume of emails received from each address in our training data.

To begin to explore how this scaling affects our first feature, we will need to count the number of times each email address appears in our data. To do this, we will use the `plyr` package, which we have already loaded in as a dependency for `ggplot2`. If you worked through the example in Chapter 1, then you have already seen `plyr` in action.

Briefly, the family of functions in `plyr` are used to chop data into smaller squares and cubes so that we can operate over these pieces all once. (This is very similar to the popular Map-Reduce paradigm used in many large-scale data analysis environments.) Here, we will be performing a very simple task: find all of the columns with matching addresses in the `From.EMail` column and count them.

To do this, we use the `ddply` function, which operates on data frames, with our training data. The syntax has us define the data grouping we want first—which in this case in only the `From.EMail` dimension—then the operation we will run over that grouping. Here, we will use the `summarise` option to create a new column named `Freq` with the count information. You can use the `head(from.weight)` command to inspect the results:

```
from.weight <- ddply(priority.train, .(From.EMail), summarise, Freq=length(Subject))
```

 In this case, the operation asks for the `length` of the vector at column `Subject` in the chopped up data frame, but we could have actually used any column name from the training data to get the same result, because all columns matching our criteria will have the same length. Becoming more familiar with `plyr` for manipulating data will be extremely valuable to you going forward, and we highly recommend the package author's documentation [HW11].

To get a better sense of the scale of this data, let's plot the results. Figure 4-2 shows a bar chart of the volume of emails from users who have sent more than six emails. We have performed this truncation to make it easier to read, but even with this data removed, we can already see how quickly the data scales. The top emailer, `tim.one@comcast.ent`, has sent 45 messages in our data. That's about 15 times more emails than the average person in our training data! But `tim.one@comcast.ent` is pretty unique. As you can see from Figure 4-2, there are only a few other senders near his level, and the frequency drops off very quickly after them. How could we weight an observation from an average person in our training data without skewing that value to account for outliers like our top emails?

A Log-Weighting Scheme

The answer comes in transforming the scales. We need to make the numerical relationship among the units in our feature set less extreme. If we compare the absolute frequency counts, then an email from `tim.one@comcast.ent` will be weighted as 15 times more important than email from an average sender. This is very problematic, as we will eventually want to establish a threshold for being either priority or not based on the range of weight values produced by our ranker at the learning stage. With such extreme skewness, our threshold will either be far too low or far too high, so we need to rescale the units in order to account for the nature of our data.

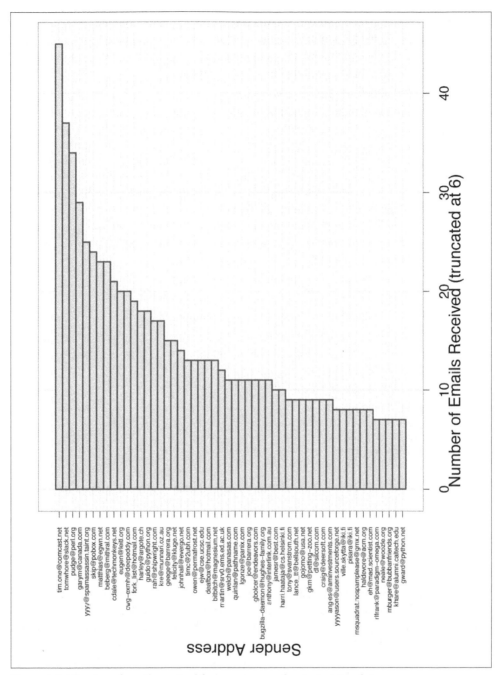

Figure 4-2. Number of emails received from various senders in training data

This brings us to *logarithms* and log-transformations. You are probably familiar with logarithms from elementary mathematics, but if not, the concept is quite simple. A logarithm is a function that returns the exponent value that would satisfy an equation where some base number is being raised to that exponent equals the number given to the logarithmic function.

The base value in a log-transformation is critical. As hackers, we are familiar with thinking of things in base two, or *binary*. We may very easily construct a log-transformation of base two. In this case, we would solve an equation for the exponent value where the input value is equal to two raised to that exponent. For example, if we transformed 16 by log base-two, it would equal four, because two raised to the 4th power equals 16. In essence, we are "reversing" an exponential, so these types of transformations work best when the data fit such a function.

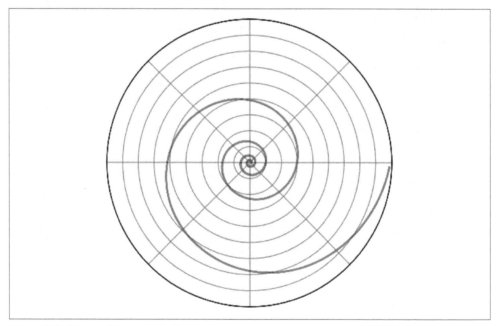

Figure 4-3. A natural-log spiral, often observed in nature

The two most common log-transformations are the so-called *natural log* and the *log base-10* transformation. In the former, the base is the special value *e*, which is an irrational constant (like *pi*) equal to approximately 2.718. The name *natural log* is often denoted ln. Rates of change equal to this constant are very often observed in nature, and in fact the derivation can be done geometrically as a function of the angles inside a circle. You are likely very familiar with shapes and relationships that follow a natural log, although you may not have thought of them in these terms. Figure 4-3 illustrates a natural log spiral, which can be observed in many naturally-occurring phenomenon. Some examples include the interior structure of a nautilus shell, the spiraling winds of a hurricane (or tornado)—even the scattering of interstellar particles in our galaxy follow a natural logarithmic spiral. Also, many professional camera settings' apertures are set to vary by natural logs.

Given the intimate relationship between this value and many naturally occurring phenomena, it is a great function for re-scaling social data—like email activity—that is exponential. Alternatively, the log base-10 transformation, often denoted log10, replaces the e value in the natural log-transform with a 10. Given how log-transforms work, we know that the log base-10 transformation will reduce large values to much smaller ones than the natural log. For example, the log base-10 transformation of 1,000 is 3; because 10 raised to the third is 1,000, while the natural log is approximately 6.9. Therefore, it makes sense to use a log base-10 transformations when our data scale by a very large exponent.

The ways in which both of these options would transform our email volume data are illustrated in Figure 4-4. In this figure, we can see that the volume of emails sent by the users in the training data follows a fairly steep exponential. By transforming those values by the natural log and log base-10, we significantly flatten out that line. As we know, the log base-10 transforms the values substantially, while the natural log still provides some variation that would allow us to pull out meaningful weights from this training data. For this reason, we will use the natural log to define the weight for our email volume feature:

```
from.weight <- transform(from.weight, Weight=log(Freq + 1))
```

 As we have done here, and as we explained in detail in Chapter 2, it is always a good idea to explore your data visually as you are working through any machine learning problem. We want to know how all of the observations in our feature set relate to one another in order to make the best predictions. Often, the best way to do this is through data visualization.

Finally, recall from grade school mathematics your rules for exponents. Anything raised to zero always equals one. This is very important to keep in mind when using log-transformation in a weighting scheme, because any observation equal to one will be transformed to zero. This is problematic in a weighting scheme, because multiplying other weights with zero will zero out the entire value. To avoid this, **we always add one to all observations before taking logs**.

 There is actually a function in R called log1p that computes log(1 + p), but for the purposes of learning and being explicit we will do this addition "by hand."

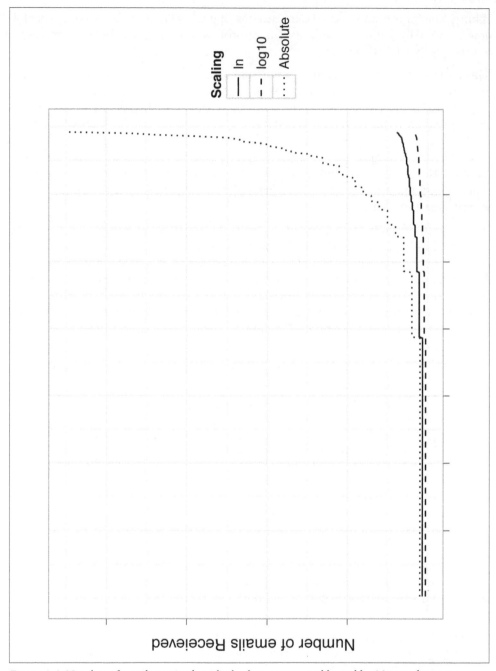

Figure 4-4. Number of emails received, with absolute counts, and ln and log10 transformation

Given the rescaling, this does not affect our results, and it keeps all weights greater than zero. In this case, we are using the default base value for the log function, which is the natural log.

 For our purposes we will never have an observation in our feature set that is equal to zero, because we are counting things. If there are no observations of something, then it simply doesn't enter our training data. In some cases, however, this will not be true, and you may have zero observations in your data. The log of zero is undefined, and if you try to compute it in R, it will return the special value -Inf. Often, having instances of -Inf in your data with cause things to blow up.

Weighting from Email Thread Activity

The second feature we want to extract from the data is email thread activity. As noted, we have no way of knowing whether the user we are building this ranking for has responded to any emails, but we can group messages by their thread and measure how active they have been since they started. Again, our assumption in building this feature is that time is important, and therefore threads that have more messages sent over a short period of time are more active and consequently more important.

The emails in our data set do not contain specific thread IDs, but a logical way to identify threads within the training data is to look for emails with a shared subject line. That is, if we find a subject that begins with "re: ", then we know that this is part of some thread. When we see a message like this, we can look around for other messages in that thread and measure the activity.

```
find.threads <- function(email.df) {
    response.threads <- strsplit(email.df$Subject, "re: ")
    is.thread <- sapply(response.threads, function(subj) ifelse(subj[1] == "",
                                                                TRUE,
                                                                FALSE))
    threads <- response.threads[is.thread]
    senders <- email.df$From.EMail[is.thread]
    threads <- sapply(threads, function(t) paste(t[2:length(t)], collapse="re: "))
    return(cbind(senders,threads))
}

threads.matrix<-find.threads(priority.train)
```

This is precisely what the find.threads function attempts to do with our training data. If we split every subject in our training data by "re:", then we can find threads by looking for split character vectors with an empty character as the first element. Once we know which observations in the training data are part of threads, we can extract the senders from those threads and the subject. The result matrix will have all of the senders and initial thread subject in our training data.

```
email.thread <- function(threads.matrix) {
    senders <- threads.matrix[, 1]
    senders.freq <- table(senders)
```

```
    senders.matrix <- cbind(names(senders.freq), senders.freq, log(senders.freq + 1))
    senders.df <- data.frame(senders.matrix, stringsAsFactors=FALSE)
    row.names(senders.df) <- 1:nrow(senders.df)
    names(senders.df) <- c("From.EMail", "Freq", "Weight")
    senders.df$Freq <- as.numeric(senders.df$Freq)
    senders.df$Weight <- as.numeric(senders.df$Weight)
    return(senders.df)
  }

  senders.df <- email.thread(threads.matrix)
```

Now, we will create a weighting based on the senders who are most active in threads. This will be a supplement to the volume-based weighting we just did for the entire data set, but now we will focus only on those senders present in the threads.matrix. The function email.thread will take the threads.matrix as input and generate this secondary volume-based weighting. This will be very similar to what we did in the previous section, except this time we will use the table function to count the frequency of senders in the threads. This is done simply to show a different method for accomplishing the same calculation on a matrix in R, rather than a data frame using plyr. Most of this function simply performs housekeeping on the senders.df data frame, but notice that we are again using a natural-log weighting.

As the final piece to the email thread feature, we will create a weighting based on threads that we know are active. We have already identified all of the threads in our training data and created a weighting based on the terms in those threads. Now, we want to take that knowledge and give additional weight to known threads that are also active. The assumption here is that if we already know the threads, we expect a user to place more importance on those threads that are more active.

Using the threads.matrix we just created, we will go back into the training data to find all of the emails inside each thread. To do this, we create the get.threads function, which will take the threads.matrix and out training data as arguments. Using the unique command, we create a vector of all thread subjects in our data. Now we need to take this information and measure each thread's activity:

```
  get.threads <- function(threads.matrix, email.df) {
    threads <- unique(threads.matrix[, 2])
    thread.counts <- lapply(threads, function(t) thread.counts(t, email.df))
    thread.matrix <- do.call(rbind, thread.counts)
    return(cbind(threads, thread.matrix))
  }

  thread.counts <- function(thread, email.df) {
    thread.times <- email.df$Date[which(email.df$Subject == thread
    | email.df$Subject == paste("re:", thread))]
    freq <- length(thread.times)
    min.time <- min(thread.times)
    max.time <- max(thread.times)
    time.span <- as.numeric(difftime(max.time, min.time, units="secs"))
    if(freq < 2) {
        return(c(NA,NA,NA))
```

```
    }
    else {
        trans.weight <- freq / time.span
        log.trans.weight <- 10 + log(trans.weight, base=10)
        return(c(freq,time.span, log.trans.weight))
    }
}

thread.weights <- get.threads(threads.matrix, priority.train)
thread.weights <- data.frame(thread.weights, stringsAsFactors=FALSE)
names(thread.weights) <- c("Thread","Freq","Response","Weight")
thread.weights$Freq <- as.numeric(thread.weights$Freq)
thread.weights$Response <- as.numeric(thread.weights$Response)
thread.weights$Weight <- as.numeric(thread.weights$Weight)
thread.weights <- subset(thread.weights, is.na(thread.weights$Freq) == FALSE)
```

The `thread.counts` functions will do this. Using the thread subject and training data as parameters, we will collect all of the date and time stamps for all emails matching the thread in the `thread.times` vector. We can measure how many emails have been received in training data for this thread by measuring the length of `thread.times`.

Finally, to measure the activity level, we need to know how long the thread has existed in our training data. Implicitly, there is truncation on either side of this data. That is, there may be emails that were received in a thread before our training data started or after. There is nothing we can do about this, so we will take the minimum and maximum date/times for each thread and use these to measure the timespan. The function `diff time` will calculate the amount of time elapsed between two POSIX objects in some units. In our case, we want the smallest unit possible: seconds.

Due to the truncation, it may be that we observe only a single message in a thread. This could be a thread that ended just as the training data got collected or just started when collection ended. Before we can create a weight based on the activity over the timespan of a thread, we must flag those threads for which we have only one message. The if-statement at the end of `thread.counts` does this check and returns a vector of `NA` if the current thread has only one message. We will use this later to scrub these from the activity weighting data.

The final step is to create a weighting for those messages we can measure. We start by calculating the ratio of messages-to-seconds elapsed in the thread. So, if a message were sent every second in a given thread, the result would be one. Of course, in practice, this number is much lower, with the average number of messages in each thread about 4.5 and the average elapsed time about 31,000 seconds (8.5 hours). Given these scales, the vast majority of our ratios are tiny fractions. As before, we still want to transform these values using logs, but because we are dealing with fractional values, this will result in negative numbers. We cannot have a negative weight value in our scheme, so we will have to perform an additional transformation that is formally called an *affine transformation*.

An affine transformation is simply a linear movement of points in space. Imagine a square drawn on piece of graph paper. If you wanted to move that square to another position on the paper, you could do so by defining a function that moved all of the points in the same direction. This is an affine transformation. To get non-negative weights in `log.trans.weight`, we will simply add 10 to all the log-transformed values. This will insure that all of the values will be proper weights with a positive value.

As before, once we have generated the weight data with the `get.threads` and `thread.counts`, we will perform some housekeeping on the `thread.weights` data frame to keep the naming consistent with the other weight data frames. In the final step, we use the `subset` function to remove any rows that refer to threads with only one message (i.e., *truncated* threads). We can now use `head(thread.weights)` to check the results:

```
head(thread.weights)
                                    Thread Freq Response    Weight
1         please help a newbie compile mplayer :-)    4    42309 5.975627
2                        prob. w/ install/uninstall    4    23745 6.226488
3                                http://apt.nixia.no/   10   265303 5.576258
4            problems with 'apt-get -f install'    3    55960 5.729244
5                    problems with apt update    2     6347 6.498461
6 about apt, kernel updates and dist-upgrade    5   240238 5.318328
```

The first two rows are good examples of how this weighting scheme values thread activity. In both of these threads, there have been four messages. The `prob. w/ install/uninstall` thread, however, has been in the data for about half as many seconds. Given our assumptions, we would think that this thread is more important and therefore should have a higher weight. In this case, we give messages form this thread about 1.04 times more weight than those from the `please help a newbie compile mplayer :-)` thread. This may or may not seem reasonable to you and therein lies part of the art in designing and applying a scheme such as this to a general problem. It may be that in this case, our user would not value things this way (while others might), but because we want a general solution, we must accept the consequences of our assumptions.

The final weighting data we will produce from the threads are the frequent terms in these threads. Similar to what we did in Chapter 3, we create a general function `term.counts` that takes a vector of terms and a `TermDocumentMatrix` control list to produce the TDM and extract the counts of terms in all of the threads. The assumption in creating this weighting data is that frequent terms in active thread subjects are more important than terms that are either less frequent or not in active threads. We are attempting to add as much information as possible to our ranker in order to create a more granular stratification of emails. To do so, rather than look only for already-active threads, we want to also weight threads that "look like" previously active threads, and *term weighting* is one way to do this:

```
term.counts <- function(term.vec, control) {
    vec.corpus <- Corpus(VectorSource(term.vec))
    vec.tdm <- TermDocumentMatrix(vec.corpus, control=control)
    return(rowSums(as.matrix(vec.tdm)))
}
```

```
thread.terms <- term.counts(thread.weights$Thread,
  control=list(stopwords=stopwords()))
thread.terms <- names(thread.terms)

term.weights <- sapply(thread.terms,
  function(t) mean(thread.weights$Weight[grepl(t, thread.weights$Thread,
              fixed=TRUE)]))
term.weights <- data.frame(list(Term=names(term.weights), Weight=term.weights),
  stringsAsFactors=FALSE, row.names=1:length(term.weights))
```

The final weighting data we will build is based on term frequency in all email messages in the training data. This will proceed almost identically to our method for counting terms in the spam classification exercise; however, this time we will assign log-transformed weights based on these counts. As with the term-frequency weighting for thread subjects, the implicit assumption in the msg.weights data frame is that a new message that looks like other messages we have seen before is more important than a message that is totally foreign to us:

```
msg.terms <- term.counts(priority.train$Message,
    control=list(stopwords=stopwords(),
    removePunctuation=TRUE, removeNumbers=TRUE))

msg.weights <- data.frame(list(Term=names(msg.terms),
    Weight=log(msg.terms, base=10)), stringsAsFactors=FALSE,
    row.names=1:length(msg.terms))

msg.weights <- subset(msg.weights, Weight > 0)
```

We now have five weight data frames with which to perform our ranking! This includes from.weight (social activity feature), senders.df (sender activity in threads), thread.weights (thread message activity), term.weights (terms from active threads), and msg.weights (common terms in all emails). We are now ready to run our training data through the ranker to find a threshold for marking a message as important.

Training and Testing the Ranker

To generate a priority rank for each message in our training data, we must multiply all of the weights produced in the previous section. This means that for each message in the data, we will need to parse the email, then take the extracted features and match them to corresponding weight data frames to get the appropriate weighting value. We will then take the product of these values to produce a single—and unique—rank value for each message. The rank.message function below is a single function that takes a file path to a message and produces a priority ranking for that message based on the features we have defined and their subsequent weights. The rank.message function relies on many functions we have already defined, as well as a new function, get.weights (which does the weight lookup when the feature does not map to a single weight—i.e., subject and message terms):

```
get.weights <- function(search.term, weight.df, term=TRUE) {
    if(length(search.term) > 0) {
        if(term) {
            term.match <- match(names(search.term), weight.df$Term)
        }
        else {
            term.match <- match(search.term, weight.df$Thread)
        }
        match.weights <- weight.df$Weight[which(!is.na(term.match))]
        if(length(match.weights) > 1) {
            return(1)
        }
        else {
            return(mean(match.weights))
        }
    }
    else {
        return(1)
    }
}
```

We first define get.weights, which takes three arguments: some search terms (a string), the weight data frame in which to do the look up, and a single Boolean value term. This final parameter will allow us to tell the application if it is doing a lookup on a term data frame or on a thread data frame. We will treat these lookups slightly differently due to differences in column labels in the thread.weights data frame, so we need to make this distinction. The process here is fairly straightforward, as we use the match function to find the elements in the weight data frame that match search.term and return the weight value. What is more important to notice here is how the function is handling non-matches.

First, we do one safety check to be sure that the search term being passed to get.weights is valid by checking that it has some positive length. This is the same type of check we performed while parsing the email data to check that an email actually had a subject line. If it is an invalid search term, then we simply return a 1 (which elementary mathematics tells us will not alter the product computed in the next step because of the rules for multiplication by 1). Next, the match function will return an NA value for any elements in the search vector that do not match search.term. Therefore, we extract the weight values for only those matched elements that are not NA. If there are no matches, the term.match vector will be all NA's, in which case match.weights will have a zero length. So, we do an additional check for this case, and if we encounter this case we again return 1. If we have matched some weight values, we return the mean of all these weights as our result.

The rank.message function uses similar rules to the get.weights function for assigning weight values to the features extracted from each email in the data set. First, it calls the parse.email function to extract the four features of interest. It then proceeds to use a series of if-then clauses to determine whether any of the features extracted from the current email are present in any of the weight data frames used to rank and assigns weights appropriately. The `from` and `thread.from` use the social interaction features to find weight based on the sender's email address. Note that, in both cases, if the `ifelse` function does not match anything in the data weight data frames, a 1 is returned. This is the same strategy implemented in the `get.weights` function:

```
rank.message <- function(path) {
    msg <- parse.email(path)
    # Weighting based on message author

    # First is just on the total frequency
    from <- ifelse(length(which(from.weight$From.EMail == msg[2])) > 0,
        from.weight$Weight[which(from.weight$From.EMail == msg[2])], 1)

    # Second is based on senders in threads, and threads themselves
    thread.from <- ifelse(length(which(senders.df$From.EMail == msg[2])) > 0,
        senders.df$Weight[which(senders.df$From.EMail == msg[2])], 1)

    subj <- strsplit(tolower(msg[3]), "re: ")
    is.thread <- ifelse(subj[[1]][1] == "", TRUE, FALSE)
    if(is.thread) {
        activity <- get.weights(subj[[1]][2], thread.weights, term=FALSE)
    }
    else {
        activity <- 1
    }

    # Next, weight based on terms

    # Weight based on terms in threads
    thread.terms <- term.counts(msg[3], control=list(stopwords=stopwords()))
    thread.terms.weights <- get.weights(thread.terms, term.weights)

    # Weight based terms in all messages
    msg.terms <- term.counts(msg[4], control=list(stopwords=stopwords(),
        removePunctuation=TRUE, removeNumbers=TRUE))
    msg.weights <- get.weights(msg.terms, msg.weights)

    # Calculate rank by interacting all weights
    rank <- prod(from, thread.from, activity,
        thread.terms.weights, msg.weights)

    return(c(msg[1], msg[2], msg[3], rank))
}
```

For the thread- and term-based weighting, some internal text parsing is done. For threads, we first check that the email being ranked is part of a thread in the exact same way we did during the training phase. If it is, we look up a rank; otherwise, we assign 1. For term-based weighting, we use the `term.counts` function to get the terms of interest from the email features and then weight accordingly. In the final step, we generate the `rank` by passing all of the weight values we have just looked up to the `prod` function. The `rank.message` function then returns a vector with the email's data/time, sender's address, subject, and rank.

We are now ready to fire up our ranker! Before we can proceed, we will split our data into two chronologically divided sets. The first will be the training data, which we call `train.paths`. We will use the ranking data generated from here to establish a threshold value a "priority" message. Once we have this, we can run the ranker over the emails in `test.paths` to determine which ones are priority and to estimate their internal rank ordering. Next, we will apply the `rank.messages` function to the `train.paths` vector to generate a list of vectors containing the features and priority rank for each email. We then perform some basic housekeeping to convert this list to a matrix. Finally, we we convert this matrix to a data frame with column names and properly-formatted vectors:

```
train.paths <- priority.df$Path[1:(round(nrow(priority.df) / 2))]
test.paths <- priority.df$Path[((round(nrow(priority.df) / 2)) + 1):nrow(priority.df)]

train.ranks <- lapply(train.paths, rank.message)
train.ranks.matrix <- do.call(rbind, train.ranks)
train.ranks.matrix <- cbind(train.paths, train.ranks.matrix, "TRAINING")
train.ranks.df <- data.frame(train.ranks.matrix, stringsAsFactors=FALSE)
names(train.ranks.df) <- c("Message", "Date", "From", "Subj", "Rank", "Type")
train.ranks.df$Rank <- as.numeric(train.ranks.df$Rank)

priority.threshold <- median(train.ranks.df$Rank)

train.ranks.df$Priority <- ifelse(train.ranks.df$Rank >= priority.threshold, 1, 0)
```

 You may notice that `train.ranks <- lapply(train.paths, rank.mes sage)` causes R to throw a warning. This is not a problem, but simply a result of the way we have built the ranker. You may wrap the `lapply` call in the `suppressWarnings` function if you wish to turn off this warning.

We now perform the critical step of calculating a threshold value for priority email. As you can see, for this exercise we have decided to use the median rank value as our threshold. Of course, we could have used many other summary statistics for this threshold, as we discussed in Chapter 2. Because we are not using pre-existing examples of how emails ought to be ranked to determine this threshold, we are performing a task that is not really a standard sort of supervised learning. But we have chosen the median for two principled reasons. First, if we have designed a good ranker, then the ranks should have a smooth distribution, with most emails having low rank and many fewer emails having a high rank. We are looking for "important emails," i.e., those that are most unique or unlike the normal flow of email traffic. Those will be the emails in the right-tail of the rank distribution. If this is the case, those values greater than the median will be those somewhat greater than the typical rank. Intuitively, this is how we want to think about recommending priority email: those with rank larger than the typical email.

Second, we know that the test data will contain email messages that have data that does not match anything in our training data. New emails are flowing in constantly, but given our setup, we have no way of updating our ranker. As such, we may want to have a rule about priority that is more inclusive than exclusive. If not, we may miss messages that are only partial matches to our features. Finally, we add a new binary column `Priority` to `train.ranks.df` indicating whether the email will be recommended as priority by our ranker.

Figure 4-5 shows the density estimate for the ranks calculated on our training data. The vertical dashed line is the median threshold, which is about 24. As you can see, our ranks are very heavy-tailed, so we have created a ranker that performs well on the training data. We can also see that the median threshold is very inclusive, with a large portion of the downward sloping density included as priority email. Again, this is done intentionally. A much less inclusive threshold would be to use the standard deviation of the distributions, which we can calculate with `sd(train.ranks.df$Rank)`. The standard deviation is about 90, which would almost exactly exclude any emails outside of the tail.

We will now calculate the rank values for all of the emails in our test set. This process proceeds exactly the same way as it did for our training data, so we will not reproduce the code here to save space. To see the code, refer to the "code/priority_inbox.R" file included for this chapter at about line 308. Once we have calculated the ranks for the test data, we can compare the results and see how well our ranker did on new emails.

Figure 4-6 overlays the density of ranks from the test data on the densities in Figure 4-5. This illustration is very informative regarding the quality of our ranker. First, we notice that there is much more density in the test data at the very low end of the distributions. This means that there are many more emails with a low rank. Additionally, the test density estimate is much less smooth than the training data. This is evidence that the test data includes many observations not in our training data. Because these observations do not match anything in our training data, the ranker effectively ignores this information.

While this is problematic, we avoid disaster because we used an inclusive threshold for priority email. Note that there is still a reasonable amount of density for the test data to the right of the threshold line. This means our ranker was still able to find emails to recommend as important from the test data. As a final check, let's actually see which emails our ranker pushed to the top.

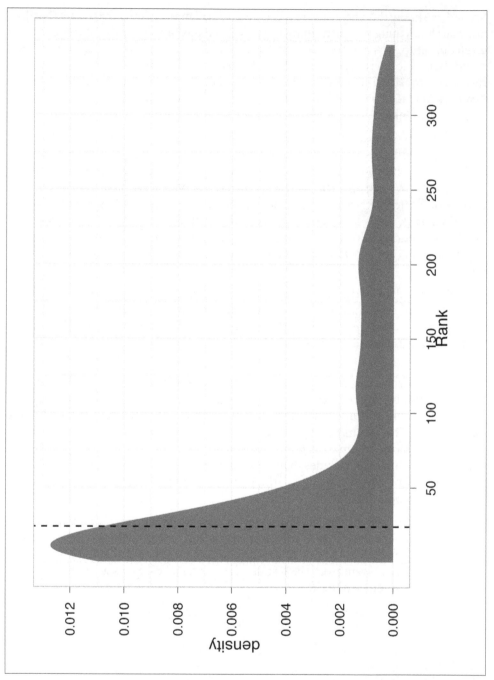

Figure 4-5. Density of weights in training data, with priority threshold as 1 standard deviation of weights

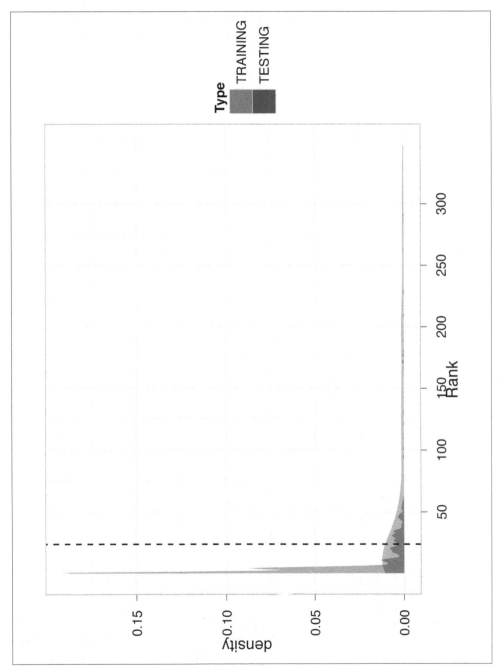

Figure 4-6. Density of weights for test data overlaid on training data density

There is an inherent "unknowable" quality to creating a ranker of this type. Throughout this entire exercise, we have posted assumptions about each feature we included in our design and attempted to justify these intuitively. However, we can never know the "ground truth" as to how well our ranker is doing, because we can't go back and ask the user for whom these emails were sent if the ordering is good or makes sense. In the classification exercise, we knew the labels for each email in the training and test set, so we could measure explicitly how well the classifier was doing using the confusion matrix. In this case we can't, but we can try to infer how well the ranker is doing be looking at the results. This is what makes this exercise something distinct from standard supervised learning.

Table 4-1 shows the 10 newest emails in test data that have been labeled as priority by our ranker. The table is meant to mimic what you might see in your email inbox if you were using this ranker to perform priority inbox over your emails with the added information of the email's rank. If you can excuse some of the somewhat odd or controversial subject headings, we'll explore these results to check how the ranker is grouping emails.

Table 4-1. Results of priority inbox testing

Date	From	Subject	Rank
12/1/02 21:01	geege@barrera.org	RE: Mercedes-Benz G55	31.97963566
11/25/02 19:34	deafbox@hotmail.com	Re: Men et Toil	34.7967621
10/10/02 13:14	yyyy@spamassassin.taint.org	Re: [SAdev] fully-public corpus of mail available	53.94872021
10/9/02 21:47	quinlan@pathname.com	Re: [SAdev] fully-public corpus of mail available	29.48898756
10/9/02 18:23	yyyy@spamassassin.taint.org	Re: [SAtalk] Re: fully-public corpus of mail available	44.17153847
10/9/02 13:30	haldevore@acm.org	Re: From	25.02939914
10/9/02 12:58	jamesr@best.com	RE: The Disappearing Alliance	26.54528998
10/8/02 23:42	harri.haataja@cs.helsinki.fi	Re: Zoot apt/openssh & new DVD playing doc	25.01634554
10/8/02 19:17	tomwhore@slack.net	Re: The Disappearing Alliance	56.93995821
10/8/02 17:02	johnhall@evergo.net	RE: The Disappearing Alliance	31.50297057

What's most encouraging about these results is that the ranker is grouping threads together very well. You can see several examples of this in the table, where emails from the same thread have all been marked as priority and are grouped together. Also, the ranker appears to be giving appropriately high ranks to emails from frequent senders, as is the case for outlier senders such as `tomwhore@slack.net` and `yyyy@spamassas sin.taint.org`. Finally, and perhaps most encouraging, the ranker is making messages priority that were not present in the training data. In fact, only 12 out of the 85 threads in the test data marked as priority are continuations from the training data (about 14%). This shows that our ranker is able to apply observations from training data to new threads in the test data and make recommendations without updating. This is very good!

In this chapter we have introduced the idea of moving beyond a feature set with only one element to a more complex model with many features. We have actually accomplished a fairly difficult task, which is to design a ranking model for email when we can only see one half of the transactions. Relying on social interactions, thread activity, and common terms, we specified four features of interest and generated five weighting data frames to perform the ranking. The results, which we have just explored, were encouraging, though without *ground truth*, difficult to test explicitly.

With the last two chapters behind us, you've worked through a relatively simple example of supervised learning used to perform spam classification and a very basic form of heuristic-based ranking. We hope the experience has piqued your interest in machine learning.

Works Cited

Books

[Adl10] Adler, Joseph. *R in a Nutshell*. O'Reilly Media, 2010.

[GH06] Gelman, Andrew, and Jennifer Hill. *Data Analysis Using Regression and Multilevel/Hierarchical Models*. Cambridge University Press, 2006.

[HTF09] Hastie, Trevor, Robert Tibshirani, and Jerome Friedman. *The Elements of Statistical Learning*. Springer, 2009.

[JMR09] Jones, Owen, Robert Maillardet, and Andrew Robinson. *Introduction to Scientific Programming and Simulation Using R*. Chapman and Hall, 2009.

[Pea09] Pearl, Judea. *Causality*. Cambridge University Press, 2009.

[Seg07] Segaran, Toby. *Programming Collective Intelligence: Building Smart Web 2.0 Applications*. O'Reilly Media, 2007.

[Spe08] Spector, Phil. *Data Manipulation with R*. Springer, 2008.

[Wic09] Wickham, Hadley. *ggplot2: Elegant Graphics for Data Analysis*. Springer, 2009.

[Wil05] Wilkinson, Leland. *The Grammar of Graphics*. Springer, 2005.

Articles

[DA10] Aberdeen, Douglas, Ondrej Pacovsky, and Andrew Slater. *The Learning Behind Gmail Priority Inbox*. LCCC : NIPS 2010 Workshop on Learning on Cores, Clusters and Clouds, 2010. *http://research.google.com/pubs/archive/36955.pdf*.

[HW11] Wickham, Hadley. *The Split-Apply-Combine Strategy for Data Analysis*. Journal of Statistical Software, April, 2011.

[LF08] Ligges, Uwe, and John Fox. *R help desk: How can I avoid this loop or make it faster?*. May 2008. *http://www.r-project.org/doc/Rnews/Rnews_2008-1.pdf*.

[SR08] Stross, Randall. *What Has Driven Women Out of Computer Science?*. The New York Times, November 15, 2008.

About the Authors

Drew Conway is a PhD candidate in politics at NYU. He studies international relations, conflict, and terrorism using the tools of mathematics, statistics, and computer science in an attempt to gain a deeper understanding of these phenomena. His academic curiosity is informed by his years as an analyst in the U.S. intelligence and defense communities.

John Myles White is a Ph.D. student in the Princeton Psychology Department, where he studies how humans make decisions both theoretically and experimentally. Outside of academia, John has been heavily involved in the data science movement, which has pushed for an open source software approach to data analysis. He is also the lead maintainer for several popular R packages, including ProjectTemplate and log4r.

Get even more for your money.

Join the O'Reilly Community, and register the O'Reilly books you own. It's free, and you'll get:

- $4.99 ebook upgrade offer
- 40% upgrade offer on O'Reilly print books
- Membership discounts on books and events
- Free lifetime updates to ebooks and videos
- Multiple ebook formats, DRM FREE
- Participation in the O'Reilly community
- Newsletters
- Account management
- 100% Satisfaction Guarantee

Signing up is easy:

1. Go to: oreilly.com/go/register
2. Create an O'Reilly login.
3. Provide your address.
4. Register your books.

Note: English-language books only

To order books online:
oreilly.com/store

For questions about products or an order:
orders@oreilly.com

To sign up to get topic-specific email announcements and/or news about upcoming books, conferences, special offers, and new technologies:
elists@oreilly.com

For technical questions about book content:
booktech@oreilly.com

To submit new book proposals to our editors:
proposals@oreilly.com

O'Reilly books are available in multiple DRM-free ebook formats. For more information:
oreilly.com/ebooks

Spreading the knowledge of innovators   oreilly.com

©2010 O'Reilly Media, Inc. O'Reilly logo is a registered trademark of O'Reilly Media, Inc. 00000

The information you need, when and where you need it.

With Safari Books Online, you can:

Access the contents of thousands of technology and business books

- Quickly search over 7000 books and certification guides
- Download whole books or chapters in PDF format, at no extra cost, to print or read on the go
- Copy and paste code
- Save up to 35% on O'Reilly print books
- **New!** Access mobile-friendly books directly from cell phones and mobile devices

Stay up-to-date on emerging topics before the books are published

- Get on-demand access to evolving manuscripts.
- Interact directly with authors of upcoming books

Explore thousands of hours of video on technology and design topics

- Learn from expert video tutorials
- Watch and replay recorded conference sessions

Lightning Source UK Ltd.
Milton Keynes UK
UKHW031229260121
377698UK00004B/215